MY UNCENSORED YEAR IN ITALY

Zia Wesley

Wanderlust Press
Mill Valley, California
www.notesfromabroad.biz

This is a memoir and not a work of fiction. Names, characters, places, and incidents are all real with the exception of three characters whose names the author changed to preserve their privacy.

Cover design by Barb Demarco

Notes from a Broad: My Uncensored Year in Italy / Zia Wesley — 1st ed.
ISBN 978-0-692-17853-9

ACKNOWLEDGEMENTS

I wish to thank all of my family members and friends who encouraged me to take this trip and then write about it, especially my daughter, Ariane, who is my biggest supporter, Ray and Carla who gave me a place to live when I had none, my "twin" Mary Chase (who calls me the "evil one") my first editor and dear friend Sean Murphy, my granddaughter and copy editor, Ceilidh Wolfe, and my final editor, Valerie Andrews who made me tell the whole truth. My deepest gratitude belongs to the amazing people I met in Italy, Greece, Luxembourg and Turkey, without whom there would have been no story at all.

INTRODUCTION

—— ✦✦◆✦✦ ——

Are you a perfectly happy single woman who doesn't let her singleness stand in the way of enjoying her life? I know I was. I'd take myself out to eat, go to the movies, to music events and local bars. I felt perfectly comfortable having a drink by myself and in fact, I'd often get into interesting conversations with people -- sometimes, I'd even meet a man and agree to go on a date. I'd been single for several years but, there was one thing I refused to consider doing alone; traveling abroad. The thought of flying alone didn't bother me, but wandering around a romantic city like Rome and staying in a beautiful hotel? Never! It felt sad and lonely so, I never even considered it. But the clock began to tick very loudly as my seventieth birthday approached.

When friends asked how I wanted to celebrate, I realized that all I wanted was a year in Italy and no one was about to give me that. It was my dream and dammit, if I didn't do it now, when would I? Seventy seemed HUGE to me. What was I waiting for? Well, that's easy…I was waiting for my soul partner. Duh! But he was not showing up. Tick, tock.

I thought about it for the whole year leading up to my birthday and finally made up my mind to find a way to do it before I was too old – some would say I was already too old but I was healthy, in good shape and very determined to make my dream reality. I was going to learn to speak Italian before I died if it killed me! And if it did, well, I would die knowing I hadn't missed anything. The more I thought about it, the more I realized the scary feelings were the harbinger of excitement – the thrill of the unknown – the unfamiliar rather than the familiar. What would life bring me if I stayed safely where I was? Hmmmm. I recognized that scary feeling as the precursor to adventure – stepping into the unknown is always frightening but, in my experience, it rarely turns out that way at all. In fact, the unknown had consistently provided new and wonderful experiences for me.

Coincidentally, I happened to have a broken heart and enough airline miles to fly first class to Europe...a dangerous combination. What was I waiting for again? A quick search on the net produced a little language school in the city of Cagliari on the island of Sardinia. I was shocked to discover that Sardinia was actually part of Italy -- just smaller, safer and less expensive. In fact, I could attend five full days of language school and live in a furnished one-bedroom apartment for about $300 a week – less than half of what it cost me to live in California and that included twenty hours of school a week! How could I afford NOT to go?

I decided to try it for a month. If I hated it, I could always come home. My friends told me I was brave, but I didn't feel brave at all. What I did feel were equal parts of excitement and dread and if I'd learned anything in my life, I recognized that feeling to be the precursor to possibility -- something new I could not yet imagine, the enticing unknown, a familiar seductress always quietly beckoning from a corner of my mind.

As I boarded the overseas flight to begin my new adventure, I opened my iPad to notate my thoughts about the coming journey. I am not naturally introspective in the way of most people in that I find it difficult to search my mind for insights or to figure out problems. Instead, I allow thoughts to float around willy-nilly until they suddenly come into focus in an "Ah ha!" moment. Very often, that moment follows meditation, which I have practiced for thirty years. This time, it followed two glasses of French Champagne. I saw myself seated at an outdoor café in Rome, speaking Italian to the waiter and smiled broadly.

I feel grateful for my age and the wisdom it has brought and secure in the fact that it is not an impediment in any way. I love the idea of meeting an age-appropriate man who will be at the same point in life as I am and maybe this is part of what I hope to find. Mostly, I want to embrace the unknown and trust it will reveal whatever I need to learn, to be, to do or to have going forward. Meanwhile, I write my wish list for the coming journey:

#1. Learn to speak Italian
#2. Travel around as much of Italy as possible
#3. Sing blues
#4. Visit Istanbul
#5. Sail around Greek islands on a traditional wooden *goulette*.

When I finish writing, the title, *Notes From A Broad*, pops into my mind and makes me laugh. "Well, that settles it. I'll take my usual notes and maybe end up with a book!"

At that moment, I could never have imagined exactly how fascinating travel abroad would be for a single woman of uncertain age or how educational (I became fluent in Italian and proficient in Argentine Tango), unexpectedly delightful (I enjoyed six lovers almost half my age and sang blues with bands in five countries) and nourishing (I cooked Mexican, Southern, Sicilian and California cuisines in Italy, Greece, and Luxembourg). Most importantly, I learned the meaning of what Italians call *il bel far niente* – the beauty of doing nothing which is the essence of the Italian lifestyle. It allowed me to discover a whole new attitude towards life, love, sex and relationship. I hope you'll enjoy reading about my journey and maybe even be inspired to take one of your own. Remember, it's never too late to begin anything!

Author's Note

I have taken the liberty of changing the names of a few characters and renamed my ex-boyfriend, true love, Luke. All other characters retain their true identity.

CHAPTER 1

DEPARTURE AND ARRIVAL

M y friends back in California were enjoying margaritas
in celebration of Cinco de Mayo while I recovered from
the hell of yesterday's trip. My airline miles had taken me
from New York to London, Heathrow airport where I took a
two-and-a-half-hour bus ride to Stanstead airport for an
overnight so I could catch an early morning flight to Sardinia.
I had been excited to find an inexpensive flight to Sardinia but
once onboard, realized why Ryanair is dirt-cheap: they fly
antique planes. This one may have actually been the puddle
jumper I had taken in 1962 from White Plains to Ithaca, New
York. The seats do not recline, and the flight attendant throws
back his head and laughs when I ask. The plump female
attendant is obviously aware of the fact she has outgrown her
uniform because the buttons on her jacket had been moved to
the farthest edge of the closure and secured with gigantic
safety pins in order to add an extra couple inches. Considering
this DIY tailoring, I doubt she is unaware of the split seam all
the way down the back of her skirt, beginning just below her
ample rump. Just in case, I bring this to her attention to which
she replies casually, "oh, I'll just put on my jacket" (which
ended a foot above the ripped seam and covered nothing).

Fortunately, the flight is only two hours long, so I pop in my ear buds and doze off for the duration.

Upon our arrival in Alghero, Sardinia, I am the first one off the plane and onto the Tarmac where the blast of heat and humidity surprises me. I never imagined Sardinia as a tropical island, and it makes me giddy...until I collected my luggage and head out of the air-conditioned terminal to the bus stop to wait three and a half hours for the bus taking me to the southern-most end of the island. It is a funky shelter several unpaved blocks from the small terminal, with aluminum bars for seats. Enjoyment of the tropical splendor quickly melts with the rest of me as rivulets of sweat roll down my torso beneath my long-sleeved tee shirt. In less than five minutes I am soaking wet. Since the area is basically deserted, I open my suitcase and pull out a change of clothes, using my damp tee shirt to mop myself up.

I consider returning to the terminal, but the walk back is largely uphill and even though it's broiling hot, the air seems a welcome change after the flight. To help pass the time, I crank up Paul Simon's *Graceland* album on my iPhone. No need for ear buds as no one is around. With a wild abandon fueled by being a stranger in a strange land and severe jet lag, I dance and sing to the entire album. It fells glorious! At the end, my clothes are wet again and there are still two hours left to wait. Remembering the tiny espresso bar inside the terminal as an incentive, I trudge back soaking wet and dragging my suitcases.

After inhaling a large iced café latte, a leisurely body wash in the empty restroom and another wardrobe change, I feel human again. Now there are only ninety minutes left to wait so I sit in the cool terminal and people-watch, making my way back to the bus stop just as the bus arrives. Grateful for the luxury of air-conditioning and soft velour seats, I board along with four teenaged girls on iPhones smoking hand rolled cigarettes. This makes me wonder whether they are all mixed with pot or if Sardinians simply refuse to pay the outrageous price of packaged cigarettes.

Settling into my seat for a four-hour trip following forty hours of travel, I realize I'll be arriving at 8 pm, in an unfamiliar city, met by a woman named Paola, with whom I'd only communicated via email. That would have been peachy if I had email capability on my phone. However, my contact at the language school who had arranged the pick-up had assured me that Paola would absolutely be at the terminal to meet me. Jet lagged and unable to think clearly, I focus on the scenery, intrigued by its similarity to Northern California— aside from the crumbling hill towns and castles atop every hill.

Four hours later, a mile outside the city of Cagliari, I know something is amiss when a truck towing an open two-horse trailer pulls in front of us. It's odd for horses to be brought into a city at night, I think. Except, of course, if the whole town is shut down for a festival! Seconds later, we come to a full stop as four young men in elaborate traditional costumes astride black horses trot across the roadway in front of us. I guess the costumes date back to the sixteenth or seventeenth century and wonder what the occasion might be, feeling excited—until I see the roadblocks and police. The driver pulls the bus over to the side of the road and stops because he has no other choice. Thousands of costumed pedestrians swarm everywhere on foot and horseback. The scene is totally surreal. I've been dropped into a medieval time warp and panic begins to set in as I realize we are not at any terminal or bus stop. The driver disembarks without an announcement or explanation (not that I would understand one anyway).

As I exit the bus, I ask the driver in halting Italian, "*Dove il terminale?*" (Where is the terminal?). He casually waves one arm towards the city as he lights a cigarette and explains in rapid Italian that it is not possible to go there because of the festival. "*Non e possibile,*" is easy to understand. Desperately,

I try to explain that I need directions because my friend is meeting me at the terminal.

"Call her," he suggests with a shrug of his shoulders as if I am brain dead and mimes holding a cell phone to his ear.

I shake my head rapidly saying, *"no telefono, signore."*

He regards me incredulously and repeats, *"No telefono?"* What planet was I from?

The group of teen girls, who have paused to light their cigarettes, overhear this exchange and offer me the use of one of their phones. "I don't have her number," I explain, now feeling like the idiot the driver already knows I am. "Can you email her for me?" I ask, showing the girl Paola's email address that I had written on a piece of paper. The teen types out a message that says I will be waiting on a wall in front of the port. "Where's the port?" I ask, to which the girls respond by pointing towards the sea that fronts the entire city. They wish me luck and disappear into the crowd.

I stand alone in the throng of foreign strangers with my two suitcases, a heavy travel bag slung over my shoulder and tears beginning to well in my eyes. As night descends, a feeling of dread creeps over me. I cannot see the "port" or any wall that might be in front of it. I seem to be on a main thoroughfare that at the moment, swarms with thousands of pedestrians and people on horseback. I begin to walk, pulling my suitcases behind me, but Cagliari is not a modern city with streetlights and there is no "wall" in sight. I stop to allow myself a few minutes of real tears. Unless Paola has super powers, she will never find a five-foot tall woman in the dark amidst the swarm of revelers. I need to calm down and make a new plan.

Drying my tears with the back of my hand, I take several deep breaths and decide to find a hotel for the night. I can see lights from buildings across the wide avenue and since there are no cars, easily cross the street and walk into a brightly lit pharmacy. Luckily, the young man behind the counter speaks English and twenty minutes later I am checked into the Hotel

Italia on a quaint alley two blocks above the port. (FYI, rolling suitcases are useless on thousand-year-old cobbled streets and of course, it was uphill.) After allowing myself a short pity party in an extremely expensive closet of a room, I change my clothes for the fourth time that day and head out to join the real party. The whole city is celebrating, and I might as well enjoy it. Before exiting the hotel, I stop by the front desk to ask the clerk the reason for the celebration. He explains it is the city's biggest annual event honoring Saint Efisio, who was "sort of but not really" Cagliari's patron Saint. In retrospect, this was my first hint regarding the casualness and uncertainty of all things Italian.

I walk back down the narrow, cobbled street, now much easier without my suitcases, to a busy cafe I had passed on my way up. All the tables are set outside on the wide walkway beneath a portico that runs the whole length of Via Roma, the main street of the port. My mind is set on a Negroni and I take it as a good sign that it is the first cocktail listed on the menu. A Negroni is a classic Italian cocktail composed of equal parts gin, Campari and red vermouth, garnished with slices of orange and lemon. A few minutes later, I feel revived, a little giddy and ready to eat. The hotel manager had recommended a nearby cafe where I could sit outside to watch the festivities. It is now 9:30 and a bystander tells me the parade is scheduled to begin at 10:15. I try to imagine a parade that might shut down the entire city of San Francisco beginning at that hour and even the Giants winning the World Series didn't do that! However, I am in one of the most ancient Roman Catholic cities in the world where I suppose saints are taken very seriously.

The night is balmy and from my little outdoor table the crowds are so thick that all I can see are the mounted riders, dressed in magnificent costumes straight out of an old master's painting, many with costumed women astride behind them. Enormous starched white shirts with elaborately ruffled, high collars peek out from big black wool jackets decorated

with silver or gold brocade and the women wear multiple
layered enormous skirts and equally elaborate hats with veils
that resemble mantillas. A cappella singing fills the streets and
sounds like angels as thousands of people walk or ride in
procession for the next three hours. I learn that each of the
hundreds of churches in the city has a choir in the parade;
some comprised solely of men, some all-boys and some both
male and female. All of the songs are in Latin, and they run
over and into one another as the procession makes its way
through the city in an eerie religious cacophony. I feel
transported into the past by the magical welcome to this
strange new place, which could not feel more authentically
Italian. Sometimes getting lost brings unexpected rewards,
and my first night in Italy had transformed from abject dread
into something wondrous: a once-in-a-lifetime living tableau.
My eyes fill with tears of joy this time and I enjoy a moment
of silent gratitude.

Of course, my first authentic pizza with a glass of vino
rosso is indescribably delicious. I sit at my little table until I
can no longer keep my eyes open and about one a.m. I fall into
bed and sleep until nine. An hour later, after a glorious six-
block walk along Via Roma from my hotel, I enter One World
Italiano School of Language. Five young women sit around a
desk in the reception area and one jumps up and runs to me
saying, *"Zia, Zia oh grazie dio!"* This is Paola, the woman
who was supposed to meet my bus. She hugs me hard and
speaks several rapid sentences in Italian as one of the other
women translates: "She says she was up all night worrying
about you and didn't know where you were or what to do. She
is very happy to see that you are alright."

Paola was also the woman whose home I was renting for
the first week of my stay and longer if I liked. We squeeze my
luggage into her tiny car and drive out of the city for about
eight minutes to a neighborhood easily reached by city buses
but too far to walk from the school. The neighborhood is
"new"; built in the sixties, seventies and eighties but feels

more suburban than urban. I'd hoped to be able to walk to school and wanted an area with cafes and restaurants where I would feel comfortable as a single foreign woman. But the apartment itself is very spacious and costs only one hundred-sixty Euro a week.

I hadn't realized how different Italian amenities might be until Paola begins to instruct me on how to use things in the kitchen and bathroom; the kitchen faucets are complicated and toilet paper must never be flushed but put into a separate can with a special liner/bag that has to be deposited in a special bin on the street corner. Several things make me smile like the bright orange refrigerator and the big European bathtub. In the bedroom a small alcove is entirely occupied by an old fashioned wooden drying rack for clothes. Paola instructs me to turn off the valve for the propane tank that fuels the kitchen stove before leaving the house, which makes me feel very nervous. What if I forget? Will I blow up the apartment building? She shows me how to separate the trash into the recyclables and the "bio" organic waste. There are three containers, each lined with a different type of plastic bag that must be taken outside to the corner where the communal refuse bins sit. Over the next week, I'll notice these ugly, open bins becoming filled and emptied every few days. There are similar bins throughout the city at the end of every block, unpleasant to walk by as they generally overflow and stink of garbage. However, I quickly discover how proud the Sardinians are of this system, which as I understand, is a great improvement over the former one (or lack thereof). Having lived through the garbage strike in New York City in the late sixties, I empathize.

Paola's apartment proves comfortable despite the continual wailing of stray cats in heat, but there are no cafes or restaurants in the neighborhood. So, for the first week, I eat lunch near school before returning home and either cook dinner at home or take the bus back into town to join friends. Traveling alone on the buses at night is perfectly safe but without people around, I feel lonely and some days, actually dread going home. There is so much I want to explore in the central part of the city: museums, historical sites, community events and markets and having recently left all of my friends and family, this is not a good time for me to be isolated. I need the comfort of humanity.

* * *

One World Italiano language school is located in an office building on Via Roma facing Cagliari's port and marina with lovely water views from some of the classrooms. Initially, there is only one other English-speaking student at my level; an Aussie named Annie, ten years my junior, with whom I immediately connect. She visits Cagliari regularly with her husband, John, who heads up a project at the local university. They will be in Cagliari for six weeks and return again, in the fall for another six. As I have a long way to go before I can converse in Italian, I'm grateful for English-speaking friends. There are three other beginning students, one from Russia, one from Japan, and Isabella—a twenty-year old Dane with roots in Sardinia on her father's side. Classes last an hour and a half from nine to eleven thirty followed by a twenty-minute "conversation break" downstairs at the local coffee bar. Each day during these breaks, I soothe my frustration with learning the language by trying a different version of *cornetto*, an Italian croissant, with my cappuccino. These delicious pastries are filled with either marmalade, cream, chocolate or honey and most taste too sweet. During the second week, I try the *tramezzini*, skinny, triangular shaped sandwiches on white bread without crusts; an Italian tea sandwich. I like the tuna, tomato and mayo version, which costs two euro with an accompanying tiny bag of chips, and it becomes my favorite cheap lunch.

The "conversation break" is how students meet each other to converse in Italian and where I met my other two English-speaking friends, Carole and Carys, Brits who'd previously spent time at the school. The year before, Carole had purchased a three-bedroom apartment in the little beach town of Pula, just a thirty-minute drive from Cagliari and invited me to spend the following weekend there.

I fall in love with Pula instantly. It's a small village about two kilometers from the sea with a pristine, wide white sand beach and turquoise water. It's less than a ten-minute walk from Carole's house to the village along a narrow street covered entirely by open pastel-colored umbrellas strung in rows above. There is one central piazza with four outdoor restaurants, and one church. I discover that Saint Efisio, the unofficial patron saint of Cagliari, is also the unofficial patron saint of Pula. In fact, the festival in progress on the night I arrived always begins with a procession carrying his effigy from Cagliari to Pula and ends two days later, with a procession to return it back to Cagliari! Remnants of the flowers, leaves and herbs, which are strewn like a thick blanket on the streets for the procession, still remain and I can smell their unusual earthy fragrance.

The next day, as I walk past the little church, two women are seated at a small table offering tiny bottles of something for sale. Upon inquiry, I learn that the priest and women of the town distill an essential oil from the various herbs and flowers used in the procession of Saint Efisio to sell as "home fragrance." The scent is both familiar and evocative and I buy a bottle and a "diffuser," a ceramic apparatus with a votive candle that heats the oil dispersing it into the air. Throughout the next year, I burn it in my apartment, and it becomes the scent of Cagliari to me.

Carole also introduces me to "the Hendricks Gin and Tonic" with a slice of cucumber instead of lime, for which I will be eternally grateful. Unfortunately, both Carole and Carys leave after three weeks and Annie drops out, leaving me a private student. As such, I am able to organize my schedule for afternoons, instead of mornings, which I prefer.

My new teacher, the handsome and very young Giuseppe, opens our initial (Italian) conversation with the familiar questions about where I come from, what I do for a living and how old I am. When I respond to the last query, he shakes his head no and repeats the question. I repeat my answer to which he replies "no" again and holds up his fingers to show me what I am saying. "Si" I say, nodding my head yes. His eyes widen in disbelief and he tells me to wait a moment as he pulls out his cell phone and scrolls through photos. He finds the one he is looking for and turns the phone around for me to see. It is an ancient-looking woman dressed in black with silver hair pulled into a bun, hands folded modestly in her lap. He tells me this is his nonna, his grandmother, who is exactly my age.

"Come è possibile?" he asks. How is this possible?

We have a good laugh and he becomes my new best friend.

Three weeks into this new life, I still live at Paola's and Annie invites me to a "happening" in the little neighborhood where she lives called Villanova. The event is a re-creation of the Beatles' impromptu performance on a London rooftop in the late sixties. I get lost on my way there despite my GPS and arrive at the very end to find Piazza San Domenico packed with people of all ages dressed as hippies as a very authentic Beatles cover band plays their last song on one of the rooftops. We stand on Annie's tiny balcony directly across the piazza to watch, as the bobbies appear blowing whistles and chasing away the crowds. It is magical, and I know I want to live there. It feels like home to me; a tiny community in the oldest section of the city beneath the *castello*.

The following Monday, I tell the school I need a place more centrally located and ask if they might find something in Villanova. They say there's an apartment available, but it is shared rather than single and the next day, I see it and agree to take it. It's only a ten-minute walk to school through the most picturesque streets I have ever seen anywhere and two days later, I move in. Since all I possess are my two suitcases of clothing, moving is a breeze, once we are able to squeeze them back into Paola's tiny car.

The day I move into my new apartment, the *patrona* (landlord) tells me that two other students will arrive the following day, one American and one Russian. I have mixed feelings about this but since living in Villanova is more desirable to me than living outside the city, I will deal with it. Also, the thought of built-in companions is inviting, and the American is a California girl like me named Christina. The Russian, Tanya, is a lovely young woman who speaks perfect English. As it happens, both hate their respective rooms because the beds are old sofa beds with thin mattresses and uncomfortable springs. Tanya departs without ever sleeping in hers and Christina leaves the next day. They tell the school about the unacceptable rooms and now the *patrona* will not be able to rent them to anyone else! I am paying only one hundred forty euro for a "shared" apartment that could not be shared. It is a good result for everyone (except the *patrona*) as Christina, Tanya and I become good friends anyway through our time together at school. A couple of weeks later I would be happy to have the apartment to myself to enjoy the privacy with my new lovers.

The apartment is clean and spacious and had been minimally furnished sometime in the early nineteen seventies. My bedroom is large with a brown leather couch against one wall and French glass doors that open onto a big balcony with a view of San Giovanni church whose bells rang every fifteen minutes starting at seven, making earplugs a necessity. But the apartment lacks Internet, which the *patrona* promises to remedy. She says she has "requested an appointment" and when I ask when it might be installed, gives the Italian shoulder shrug, "Eh?" (who knows) in response. It takes almost three months.

There is no mistaking six p.m. in Villanova as the church bells from San Giovanni church go completely insane for a full two minutes; first they ring six distinct bongs to indicate the time and then they bang around together for a tuneless cacophony, striking fear into the hearts of those who might consider skipping evening mass, while letting others like myself know it is time for a cocktail.

Every day here is like living in a movie; one about a single American woman in Italy, anyone that's ever been made...take your pick; *Under the Tuscan Sun; Eat, Pray, Love,* you get the picture. Two blocks from my apartment, Bar Florio is the social center of Villanova, one of the most picturesque parts of the city of Cagliari. It is a tiny place with only six bar stools and two small tables. But every day twelve bigger tables and thirty chairs are set outside in the little Piazza San Domenico. Florio begins their beverage and food service sometime in the early morning and closes sometime after one am. The handsome young owners, Andrea and Massimo, employ a large staff of servers: waiters and bar people who are very friendly and always busy. Twice a week, they manage to cram a full sized D.J. set-up inside with speakers outside and the piazza fills with dancing bodies. Live bands play outside on other nights.

Villanova is a village within a city that reminds me of the West Village in New York where I lived in the late sixties: artists, musicians, writers, politicos and everyone knows everyone else. Something different happens every day: political rallies, civic meetings, celebrations, poetry readings and fundraisers. It has become my favorite place to begin or end evenings and some nights I start and end there without ever leaving. The best pizza in Cagliari is also right next-door at Fantasma One and they allow patrons to bring their cocktails from Florio. I'd like to place a Go-Pro camera on my friend Annie's balcony above Florio for a month and set it to shoot every fifteen minutes from early morning to early morning to use as the basis for an Italian sitcom because the goings on are priceless and ever-changing: romantic trysts, arguments, hangovers, tears, family interactions, live music, opera and readings, theatrical productions, community and group events.

One evening last week I sat sipping my evening Negroni as young parents did the same while keeping half an eye on their children. A chubby little seven-year-old girl played with two younger boys running around yelling and whacking inanimate objects with sticks. When they got too loud, the father called out sharply, "Angela!" The little girl stopped in her tracks, lowered her head ever so slightly, shrugged up her shoulders and opened her palms, lifted her chin sharply and said, "Eh?" in a loud, angry voice. It is one of the classic Italian expressions that says many things, in this case, "What could you possibly want and why are you bothering me?" without any words. Italian is spoken with the whole body and it made me wonder if this is inherited genetically or learned environmentally. Angela was mimicking all the older women in her life and it was flawless. Like I said, I'm living in an Italian movie.

* * *

All women in Italy are fashion conscious and dress up to leave the house. Most of the time that means an actual dress or skirt and blouse with heels, but I'm surprised to see working and non-working women wearing very low cut and revealing blouses in the daytime, especially here in provincial Cagliari. The old adage, "If you've got it, flaunt it," seems to be the rule of thumb regardless of age. Men openly appreciate this and sometimes good-naturedly compliment a woman, but never act inappropriately. I do not adopt the low-cut look because with my curves, I'd look like a hooker. Instead, I buy several summer dresses and skirts, which prove more comfortable in the humid heat of Cagliari where air-conditioning is rarely used.

I receive lovely smiles and greetings as I walk along the street and often men are openly flirtatious but never in ways that make me feel uncomfortable or threatened. Casual dress means slacks, leggings or tailored jeans with a shirt or designer tee shirt, but true jeans are rarely seen on the streets. I wear mine proudly with tee shirts, a jean jacket and heels and with my long blonde hair, might as well have been wearing a Dayglow sign that says, "American." Since there is no chance I could ever pass for Sardinian, I happily embrace my differences.

Most of the women I meet are fiercely independent whether single or married but find it difficult to relate to my willingness to travel alone and so extensively. This strikes me as odd since travel in the EU is so unbelievably inexpensive; for about thirty dollars you can fly anywhere in Italy or to one of ten nearby countries. I think they have different priorities and travel for the sake of travel, instead of work or vacation, is not on their agendas or in their budgets. They are all educated, hard-working and more politically involved than I. During dinners or evenings at cafes, both women and men get into heated political discussions and everyone seems to be informed about specifics of events that most Americans would ignore until it was time to vote.

Each day I walk to and from school a different way to familiarize myself with my new surroundings. My favorite route includes Via Sullis, a picturesque one block long street that begins at the foot of Mussolini's Bastione Saint Remy, a soaring white marble landmark that no one credits to him out of embarrassment. Antica Cafe, one of the city's most elegant cafes, faces the Bastione on the corner. Across from the cafe's back entrance is a lovely, small two-story house behind a wrought iron gate with a steel grey BMW Z4 convertible parked in the private driveway. The upper floor has a view of the sea and I fantasize about one day living there and wonder who does. Each shop on Via Sullis is elegant and unique— from the MOMA art store to the Italian designers collective that offers local designer clothes, shoes, jewelry and fragrance. The little hair salon becomes the place where I get my hair cut and my favorite takeaway cafeteria, Mama Mia's, is one block away. A small bakery around the corner sells fresh, hot *cornetti* every morning and the elegant marble bar at Antica Cafe becomes a favorite late afternoon meeting spot for a *prosecco* with *apperitivi*. Their display of complimentary appetizers is so beautiful I photograph it. My melancholy has been vanquished by the first stage of a romantic relationship; I am falling in love with a city and feeling ecstatic.

CHAPTER 2
THE NEGRONI CHRONICLES
—— ◆◆◆◆◆ ——

Today is the tenth of June, a date I always celebrate because it's Malone's birthday, my daughter's godfather and dearest friend who died of AIDS twenty-seven years ago; way too young and entirely too soon. All these years later, he is still very present in my life – and how I wish he were here now, sipping a Negroni at Bar Florio in Piazza San Domenico, cruising all the beautiful straight men with facial hair. The image makes me smile.

I have been living in Italy for five weeks and have had more sex in the last two than I've had in the last two years. My handsome ex-lover, Vittorio, just stopped by my table to kiss me on both cheeks on his way home from his "studio" where he practices law, so it must be 7 p.m. Church bells ring every fifteen minutes here to tell me the time and fortunately, cease at ten p.m. I'm seldom asleep until many hours later as my current lover, Tonio, rarely leaves me before one; exhausted, sore and content despite a gnawing desire for my ex-boyfriend, Luke, in California. This realization brings me a rare moment of truth, filled with an emptiness I tend not to acknowledge (to myself and never to others). Were this not being notated on my iPad, the feeling would skulk back into the shadows, unnoticed. A maudlin heaviness settles around me and I know I'll sit here enveloped by it and drink alone, watching interchangeable young Italian men with beards, inhaling second hand smoke and asking myself: What the fuck I am doing? For me, reality always has two sides so on the minus side, I recognize a gnawing feeling of emptiness that I can't seem to fill with the usual distractions and my lack of progress in learning the Italian language is very frustrating; on the plus side my tango is improving, and I am living in an Italian dream in one of the most beautiful and romantic settings in the world.

* * *

I met Vittorio, my first Italian lover, one balmy summer night during the first week of living in my new apartment in the ancient and very hip neighborhood of Villanova. My ex-pat Aussie friends, Annie and John, had invited me to dinner at their house and afterwards, we walked downstairs to Bar Florio, the very lively social hub of the neighborhood. We stood outside in the tiny piazza, sipping Negronis, when one of their neighbors joined us with his friend Vittorio, a tall and classically beautiful Italian man I guessed to be in his early forties. There was obvious interest on both our parts and Annie shot me a "here's one for you" look. His eyes casually scanned me from feet to face and his interest was obvious as I am accustomed to. I say this as a matter of fact rather than pride. Men describe me as a "bombshell" (one recent lover said I look like a Playboy bunny) and no one ever guesses my age within twenty years of accuracy. Twenty-five years in the beauty industry and ten as a professional dancer, gave me beautiful skin and the stature and walk of a young athletic woman. Experience has made me certain of my sex appeal, which I am told makes me even more attractive to the opposite sex. The four of us stood around talking and drinking for over an hour until I began to fade. When I said I was going to leave, Vittorio asked where I lived.

"Just around the corner," I replied.

"I'll walk you," he offered.

Annie suppressed a squeal.

I took his arm as we strolled through the narrow, charming, cobbled streets of Villanova. When we reached my doorway, I thanked him for walking me and said goodnight to which he reacted with surprise.

"You are not going to ask me in?" he said.

"No, I don't think so," I replied with a laugh.

"But why?" he asked, seeming truly mystified.

I laugh when I'm nervous so when I stopped laughing I said, "I'm not sure why, maybe because we just met. Maybe because I haven't been with anyone for more than a year. I don't know."

Silently my mind spun in different directions; I knew how much older than him I was even if *he* didn't and how could this (way too) young man ever be the "age appropriate" mate I wished to meet. My dualistic nature rose to the surface as a familiar voice in my brain screamed, "He's gorgeous and Italian are you nuts?" I know this voice as that of a much younger woman who resides in my subconscious and will not be dissuaded.

Being a lawyer, Vittorio began to negotiate—which only made me laugh more. His English was not very good and sounded particularly funny as he tried to convince me of something he didn't really know how to say. I ended the debate by saying, "Give me your number and I'll call you after I've had a chance to think about it." Flabbergasted, he'd apparently never received such a response.

Undressing for bed I replayed the scene and asked myself why I hadn't wanted to sleep with him. It's one thing to appreciate a man's good looks but another to take the next step to physically wanting him. If we had kissed, I might have been physically turned on. The next day when I told Annie, she was appalled. "Why the hell didn't you sleep with him? He's gorgeous and smart and gainfully employed!"

"I just wasn't turned on," I said.

"Well, give him a call and another chance to flip your switch. He's perfect in my book," she said.

So that is exactly what I did: invited him to come over one night that week.

Vittorio looks like my fantasy of the perfect Italian man: about six feet two inches tall with gorgeous green eyes and thick, light brown hair flecked with silver at the temples. He has a classic, high-bridged Roman nose, prominent cheekbones and a square jaw. His long legs are beautifully muscled from running and his body is strong as well as almost hairless and deeply tanned. He is also very well endowed and yet, I felt very little sexual chemistry. What he had in physique, he lacked in sensuality and worse, he wasn't a good kisser. There was also a problem when he tried speaking English in bed. This was my first experience of sex with a non-English speaking Italian man and I soon discovered some things simply don't translate well.

As we made love, he said a couple of things that made me giggle to myself, and when he was ready to come asked breathlessly, "Can I give you my sperm?" The thought that popped into my mind was, "Why? What do you want me to do with it?" Of course, I laughed hysterically and then apologized profusely. I was looking up into the eyes of a gorgeous man who had just had a very good orgasm (are there bad ones?) and he looked perplexed and confused. It was a turn off for me and I assumed for him as well but despite my rude behavior, he wanted to see me again. Since initial encounters are rarely an accurate indication of compatibility, I agreed to give it another shot.

During our second encounter, I asked Vittorio to only speak Italian while we were making love. He had a sexy voice and I liked hearing it but, unfortunately, the lovemaking was not much better, lacking focus and sensuality and I felt zero connection. It probably didn't help the situation when I quietly sobbed afterwards—but the feeling of emptiness was so deep, the longing for what was missing in our exchange so profound, I couldn't help myself. In retrospect, I realize he was just a very immature lover.

I decided to not see him again, but he had already invited me to spend the weekend at his summerhouse in the tiny town of Bosa for an annual wine festival. Locals said Bosa was a must- see picturesque hill town on the sea and this would be a perfect way to see another part of the island, so I recruited a couple of girlfriends from school for the excursion. We would rent a car and establish our independence as just friends.

Christina, a young, voluptuous American Brunette and Isabella, a statuesque twenty-year old Dane, and I drove our rented Fiat west to the coast. It was a gorgeous summer day and we stopped at a small surfing beach (without waves) and arrived in Bosa late Saturday morning. We drove directly to the *castello* (the ancient castle) where the wine tasting began and where we would rendezvous with Vittorio, parked on a narrow street and climbed the rest of the way to the very top where we bought our tickets for ten euro each. After receiving complimentary wineglasses, trays and carrying bags, we began perusing the stalls that lined the castle walls: wines, artisanal goods; cheeses, cured meats, pickled vegetables, jams, handicrafts and jewelry. The day was sunny and warm, and we were the only English-speaking foreigners in the crowd, so we attracted a lot of attention. This was a local, small town event and everyone was curious to engage us in conversation. Italian men are flirtatious by nature and all of the younger or single men flirted openly. We were thoroughly enjoying it and had been tasting, laughing, flirting and trying out our Italian for about an hour when I spotted Vittorio and another young man perched on the castle wall. Introductions were made all around and I was surprised that his friend, Antonio (Tonio), spoke almost perfect English. Unlike Vittorio, he looked pure Sardinian (Sardo): short and dark with exotic dark slanted eyes and a shaved head. I was not particularly attracted to him but found him interesting to talk with.

For the rest of the day, the five of us made our way down Bosa's narrow, winding, cobbled streets from the castle to the town below, tasting wine and food and conversing with locals and visitors in half English half Italian. I wobbled on the cobbles in my red leather wedge sandals and Vittorio and Tonio walked on either side of me, each holding one of my arms to keep me from falling. Picture a curvaceous blonde in a tight summer dress tottering through the tiny alleyways of an ancient walled city on the arms of two young handsome Italian men. Once again, I felt like I was in an Italian film and could not have been happier. Every few minutes, old men appeared from tiny cellar doorways offering up their homemade brews that were mostly undrinkable. We swallowed to be polite and, after a couple hours, were happily inebriated. Every Italian who learned I hailed from California had the same reaction, "Why are you here when you could be there?" They knew California from movies and television and wished they could go for a visit. Many had relatives or friends who had emigrated and told me the stories of these people who were lucky enough to see such a place. I explained that was exactly how I had always felt about Italy! And they immediately understood.

As dusk began to soften the light, we arrived in Bosa's main piazza and Vittorio said he wanted to bring us to his favorite local bar. It was hidden in a tiny alley off the piazza, with two small, dark rooms (more like alcoves) filled with men. We three foreigners were the only women in the place and when I asked Vittorio if this was normal, he said, "of course. Women don't go to bars here." This was a first for me and it explained the remark made by one man as we entered, "*Ma che cazzo?*" What the fuck? A lot of the men were plainly offended and annoyed by our presence while others saw it as an invitation to make openly lewd comments. We were obviously not "local" girls or even Sardinian, so none of the usual polite rules of conduct applied. None of us (American females) had ever experienced a "men only" establishment and our Italian escorts thought it terribly amusing. By this time, we were all quite tipsy and it took a while for the reality of the situation to sink in. Had I not been inebriated, I might have felt a whole range of emotions from anger to fear. Instead I became an objective observer and simply found it interesting. So, this is what an all-male bar is like in Italy? Welcome to the provinces. We did not stay long and as we left, I wondered if the immature Vittorio thought that bringing three foreign women into that place might boost his macho image with the locals. In retrospect, I think that men who frequent "men only" establishments are rarely men who appreciate and know how to fully enjoy women.

* * *

Afterwards, we caravanned to a local supermarket to buy supplies for dinner where Tonio stayed close to me as we shopped, showing some interest and making conversation. He was very smart and well educated with an air of quiet intensity, deeper and more mature than Vittorio. As we exited the store, he mentioned something about Argentine tango, and I blurted out "Tango! Really? Do you dance?"

"Yes," he said.

"Oh, please show me," I begged.

"Show you?" he asked incredulously, "Here and now?"

"Yes, please," I pleaded, putting down the heavy bags of groceries and lifting my arms to receive him. And then something magical happened. He set his bags down and regarded me as if seeing me for the first time all day. His entire demeanor changed as he fixed me in a steady gaze and then, stepped towards me to wrap me in a tango embrace. He slowly shifted his weight from one foot to the other in preparation of his first step as I melted into his arms, then expertly moved me through the eight basic steps that begin the tango. I was hooked.

"You really dance!" I exclaimed. "Tango was one of the things I hoped to find here. Will you teach me?"

"Of course, if you are serious," he replied.

I was definitely serious about learning tango and now also seriously attracted to him. The five-minute demonstration had moved me from mild interest to heavy attraction and definitely turned me on. It was an extraordinary shift that I could not have explained at the time but would later come to understand; within the tango community, the dance is called "a fifteen-minute romance" because the intimacy required for the dance masquerades as infatuation.

* * *

Meanwhile, back at Bar Florio, it is still twilight at eight p.m. and the piazza is filled with people of all ages drinking their evening *aperitivo* as children run around playing. Andrea and Massimo, the handsome young owners, are setting up speakers and an electric keyboard outside which makes me happy because it means there will be live music to dissipate my sadness. I look around the ancient piazza and realize that I may be lacking a loving relationship, but I am in love with this place; fifty neighbors and strangers gathered outside for no other reason than to enjoy each other's company in the fading glow of soft colors on ancient buildings, the smell of pizza, the bitter orange taste of a Negroni and the cacophony of children's laughter, dogs and Italian voices. I'm just tipsy enough to feel brave and invite the handsome silver haired man standing alone to please take the empty seat at my table. After all, it's early, I am abroad, and comforted by the fact we never know what the future holds...anything might happen and in a secret corner of my heart, I hope it will. In these maudlin moments, I wonder where love is for me and if I will ever again share it with someone.

My first tango lesson with Tonio took place earlier this evening in his apartment. When we finished, he began to prepare dinner for one of his other lovers. I'm not jealous that he has sex with other women, but that he cooks for them. When I admitted this, he thought I was kidding. The pleasure I feel when a man cooks for me is equivalent to the way most women feel when being taken to an expensive restaurant. Watching a man cook me food turns me on, and I have no idea why. I only had one lover a very long time ago who really cooked for me, but I love watching a man's hands chop and stir. I like being fed. Suddenly, I dive back to my childhood where my mother was a terrible cook, and I'm watching my father make me "farmer's salad," the only childhood meal I ever thought delicious. Could this be why men preparing food makes me happy? (At the time, I did not know Tonio bought prepared food from the local market and simply warmed it up. This does not count as "preparing dinner" in my world.)

The band is warming up now...a keyboard, violinist and what else? Maybe I will get to sing tonight. My *aperitivo* plate of prosciutto, *salame*, assorted cheeses, olives and Sardinian cracker bread arrives as Vittorio reappears wearing the new neon running shoes he proudly tells me had to be ordered "special" on line because they don't carry his extra-large size here. Sigh. But there's no chemistry for me, which is lucky since he has brought a young woman, Francesca, who may be his girlfriend. She speaks almost no English, but we communicate perfectly in my broken Italian and it's a girl thing...we understand each other without words. Girlfriends are like lovers in this, I think, and by the end of the evening she and I are best friends. I can see the closeness between her and Vittorio and also her keen observations of his nature and how she calls him on things. She is clearly his intellectual equal and a lot more mature. Almost everyone seems more mature than Vittorio and he is forty-two years old!

They join my table with two other friends, and I feel happy to be surrounded by energetic young Italians. The band and vocalist begin to play and they're terrible with a maudlin sound, the audio equivalent of paint-by-numbers. They play *"That Was a Very Good Year"* and *"Fly Me to the Moon!"*

songs I disliked when I was young, and they were popular. I
wonder why they think these songs are cool or if they just like
Frank Sinatra. At their age, if they want to sound retro, they
should play David Bowie. To compensate, I drink three
Negronis and when I mispronounce it as "negrone," Francesca
lets me know how bad my mispronunciation is. It is she says,
"the N word" with an e on the end instead of the proper i.
Feeling appalled, I thank her then tell them the story of my fig
faux pas at Argiolas winery. None of them can stop laughing.
It definitely tops negroni.

My "fig faux pas": At the end of my second week in
Sardinia, I joined a group of foreigners from my language
school for a field trip to the most prestigious winery on the
island, Cantina Argiolas. Following the winemaking tour, the
twelve of us were shown into the tasting room and seated at a
lovely long wooden farm table laden with olives, cheeses,
sliced prosciutto and salami, fruits and of course, wines. With
guidance from one of the winery's expert presenters, we tasted
and nibbled for an hour. Towards the end, when the fruits were
being offered with the dessert wine, people began to share
their opinions and preferences. Carefully pulling a phrase out
of my brain in perfect Italian, I held my wine glass aloft and
proudly declared, *"Mi piace mangiare fica con questo vino."*
Everyone at the table who understood Italian froze. I surveyed
the silent guests as an elderly English woman leaned towards
me and said quietly in an upper crust British accent, "I am
afraid you've just said something raahther naahsty."

I held my breath.

"You see," she explained, "the singular word for fig is
actually slang for a woman's private part. The plural "fiche"
is always used for the actual fruit."

I had just said I enjoyed eating pussy with the dessert
wine.

Leaving my new Italian friends in hysterics, I go inside
Bar Florio to use the restroom and find my British friend Lili

seated at the bar. She asks how the wine tasting weekend in Bosa had gone.

"Fabulous and not as I'd imagined at all. I wasn't romantically interested in Vittorio anymore, but he brought his friend, Tonio along for the weekend and we've been lovers ever since. He's also teaching me tango," I say showing her Tonio's picture on my phone. Lili's jaw drops, and she asks how old he is.

"Forty-one," I reply.

"Does he know how old you are?" she asks.

"Don't be ridiculous."

She gives me a hoot and a high five and mentions they are going to a blues club afterwards. How great would that be to sing blues with an Italian band in Italy? It's another wish on my list and now I'm one step closer. I love Cagliari more every day, despite my frustration with learning the language. And just like the first stages of love, I am infatuated with the people, the city, the lifestyle and the surprises around every corner. I may not have true love or a lasting relationship but I'm learning tango and having lots of sex and that will just have to suffice for now.

CHAPTER 3
JUNE IN VILLANOVA
—— ◆◆◆◆◆ ——

Electricity in Sardinia is a continual issue and makes me realize how Americans take this everyday luxury for granted. In Italy, all structures use three types of electrical current, randomly installed in any room. Appliances have one of two types of plugs, not for any particular reason I was able to understand. For example, my hair dryer could not be plugged into the bathroom outlet where I needed to use it, but my flat iron could. On the first day in my Villanova apartment I found five electrical sockets in the bedroom. Using an adapter, I plugged in my iPad and a while later, checked to see how much of a charge it had taken to find it hadn't taken any. While attempting to unplug it, the plug was burning hot and when I gave it a gentle tug, the entire electrical socket fell out of the wall, wires and all. The next two outlets I tried to use had uneven holes that did not fit any Italian plugs or adapters in my possession. I switched on a small desk lamp plugged in next to the bed and was pleased when it lit up. But alas, that socket only took the two-pronged plug of that particular lamp and nothing else. That left one functional outlet in which I alternated charging my cell phone and iPad. It charged the devices but also heated the plugs, and I prayed they wouldn't fry every time I plugged them in.

In my next apartment, which had been newly renovated, all electrical sockets seemed to be operable. However, as I prepared my first dinner, the apartment suddenly went black. I found the fuse box using the flashlight app on my iPhone and switched it back on. Five minutes later, it shut down again, so I called the landlord, who quickly arrived to explain the dysfunctional system in this brand-new apartment. It was very simple, he explained, I just could not use a lot of appliances at once. "But I was only using the stove," I said. He walked into the bathroom and looked up at a small box near the ceiling with an illuminated red light.

"And the water heater," he said.

"The water heater?" I echoed.

He explained that, after taking a shower, washing dishes, or using the washing machine, the water heater automatically turned on (for forty minutes) to heat more water.

"But this is a newly renovated apartment'" I said, to which the landlord responded with the Italian shoulder shrug and "eh?" The New York Italians of my youth would have followed that gesture with the phrase, "Whadaya gonna do?"

I gave up using the oven because every time, regardless of how careful I was, it caused a blackout. Once, I went as far as unplugging all appliances and turning off all the lights—and it still blew.

In my last and most upscale, architecturally designed apartment, I was thrilled when my landlord said there would not be any electrical problems. For three blissful weeks, I almost felt like I was living in a first world country. But alas, one night, as my two-hour "thirty-minute eco-wash cycle" was endlessly washing, I made the mistake of popping a slice of bread into the toaster. Blackout.

At the end of my fifth week of school, I have a breakthrough day in Italian! Something clicks into place in my brain and the lesson actually makes sense. I suddenly understand everything and get a *brava* from Giuseppe. I seem to have turned a corner...and it's Friday, which has taken on a whole new meaning in my life as I remember what TGIF means. Tonight is Christina's last night before she leaves to go back to California, and we are going out on the town with all the girls. I will wear my new red fuck-me pumps (outside of my apartment) for the first time and avoid cobbled streets so I don't break my neck.

It is already full-on summer here now and I'm in full on lust. I keep wondering how I can be so physically turned on to somebody I'm not in love with and can think of no explanation other than tango. Tango is not a dance of memorization or choreographed steps. It is a shared meditation between two people connected by invisible cords between their sternums, (the breastbones). The man's role is to initiate the steps and lead the woman. The woman's role is to sense the man's intention and follow. It is a silent act of emotional and psychic communication that can only succeed if the follower (female) is able to tune out all thought – just like classic meditation practice. If a woman tries to anticipate what her partner wants rather than following, she will fail. Now that I'm dancing tango, I understand why it is called "a fifteen-minute romance"; I've been smitten by several men who would otherwise be completely unattractive to me. The magic lies in some invisible connection which we rarely feel with others, especially strangers. At a *milonga* or tango evening, men you've never met silently approach and invite you to dance. I find very few of these men attractive, but within seconds, we are standing in an intimate embrace "connecting" before they begin to move. Much of the time, I dance with my eyes closed to block out visual outside influences and facilitate my ability to feel this connection.

Yesterday's tango lesson was amazing because we'd really danced for the first time. As a former professional dancer, tango is the most difficult dance I've ever learned, and I hope you can imagine my excitement about being able to actually dance. The lesson lasted an hour and a half and ended, as Tonio said, "very unprofessionally" when he slipped his hand inside the back of my pants and caressed my ass. Clothes flew off and we had sex all over his living room and kitchen. Afterwards, I promised not to report him. If you've ever watched a professional tango performance, you no doubt described it as "sexy"—and it is. *Dancing it* is a potent aphrodisiac.

Later that night we walked to Florio for a nightcap (which Italians don't really understand) and the live music was fabulous: a gifted guitarist, and a young woman singing Bosa Nova. I drank a Campari Spritz and danced in the piazza with others until just after midnight, when they stopped playing. Tonio walked me home and left. As I lay down in bed alone, I wondered if I would ever sleep in the same bed with a man again. Luke had been the first man I ever held all night during sleep. Throughout the night, we would take turns rolling over to spoon each other, waking in the morning wrapped together. This was a total break in my pattern of sleeping "alone" on my side of the bed with my ex-husband. That may have been a way to separate and protect myself from what had become a toxic relationship. When I left him, I vowed to not sleep with any man as a way to insure I would not jump into another relationship. I did not spend a night with Luke until we had been seeing each other for a year and once I did, the level of intimacy was deeper than any I had ever known. Since our separation, sleeping alone had become difficult and I often resorted to taking an Ambien. Now, I wondered when and how that might resolve itself.

I had no expectations of what might happen during my year abroad other than a goal to learn to speak Italian well. Certainly, interesting opportunities would present themselves and I intended to stay open to all possibilities. Sometimes it's good not to have a plan and I've rarely had that luxury so, accordingly, my plan was not to have one. Here is what I know after six weeks: I am beginning to speak a little Italian, my libido is alive and well, no one cares or has any idea how old I am, I have a natural gift for dance but maybe not for learning a foreign language, I am still in love with Luke despite choosing to not be with him, I can afford to live well on Sardinia without any concern about money and I have no idea where I will be three weeks from now.

* * *

This morning I woke up wanting Tonio, a rare feeling for me as mornings have never been a favorite time for sex. My libido must be making up for the previous, post-relationship year when I chose to be celibate. Today is the first day of Tonio's two-week vacation and the first we will spend together during daylight. We planned to drive to San Antioco, a little beach town in the west, but the sky is gray and rainy. Since we are anxious to get out of the city, we decide to ignore the bad weather and bring our swimsuits along in case it clears.

We drive away from the city for over an hour with windows open to let in the damp country air, hands on each other's thighs and both turned on. Just before our destination, we turn off onto a rough dirt road towards the beach that proves impassable, stopping when we can't go any further. We turn off the engine, but the terrain is too rough to get out of the car to walk to the beach, so we recline the seats as low as they'll go and devour each other like sex-starved teenagers, climbing over the gearshift and banging our body parts against door handles and the steering wheel. When we finish, we are covered in sweat and the windows are completely steamed up. I begin to laugh and can't stop; who are we? Clothes are crumpled and snagged everywhere and Tonio can barely back the car out of the rough dirt track; the sound of brambles scraping the paint makes me cringe, but he doesn't care. How did we become so desperate?

We leave our hidden spot and head into town for lunch at a casual place he knows that only serves fried seafood;

calamari, shrimp and fish...my favorites. Everything is delicious but Tonio is always on edge when we're in public, as if he is afraid someone will see us, and it makes me uncomfortable because I don't understand why. When I ask he says that Cagliari is a small city, (more like a small town) and gossip is a main source of amusement. Everyone knows each other's business, and he prefers to fly under the radar. But it's not as if we are doing something wrong; he isn't cheating on anyone but acts as if I'm his mistress. I find his preoccupation with what others think annoying. How can a forty-year-old man live his life according to other people's standards and wishes? Is it possible to live a full life if you're constantly concerned about what other people think? For me, it goes against the essence of who I am and begins to diminish my respect for him.

After lunch we drive to the small city of Carbonia where Tonio has a short business meeting. He tells me that Mussolini built the city and as we drive in, this is immediately obvious in the monumental scale of the grey cement gateways and buildings; Mussolini's style of grandeur.

Tonio settles me into an ultra-modern café where I can drink something cool and use the Internet connection. Sipping a *café freddo*, I watch a group of teenagers clowning around outside at tables on the patio. They are very animated, table-hopping and having a good time when I notice two of them standing still and hugging. They can't be more than seventeen and the girl wears a crop top and low-slung pants. The boy is much taller than she and she clasps her hands behind his neck and leans away from him smiling. They embrace again, whispering intimately into each other's ears. Then he begins to tickle her naked back. She laughs and squirms, trying to escape, but he holds her easily with his other arm and it is delicious to watch. I imagine how she must feel to him, wriggling in his arms, her naked back beneath his strong hands and I am so happy for him. I hope it will be one of the beautiful first memories he fondly recalls when he's older. They are so very young and tasting life for the first time. Maybe this is why I'm enjoying my new lover so much, even though I don't love him...it's fresh and new and I have learned that nothing ever lasts.

* * *

As we drive home at the end of the day, Tonio tells me he wants me to meet his ex-girlfriend to see her perfect skin that is so amazing for her advanced age of fifty-nine. Can you imagine what I was thinking? She is more than a decade younger than I am and he has no idea.

The next day at school is discouraging in the manner of two steps forward and one step back. My lack of progress frustrates me, and it seems the more I learn the more insecure I am about speaking properly. In the beginning, when I was just winging it, I could bluff, fake and gesticulate my way through a communication. Now that I'm actually learning grammar, I've become afraid of saying things incorrectly and as a result, take a full minute to form one sentence, a problem I need to correct.

Of the various forms of distraction I normally use to make myself feel better, only two are available here: cooking and shopping. I decide to go shopping first and cook something comforting later. There is a red dress I have been fantasizing about in a shop window for two weeks. It is an off the shoulder, low cut sheath and every time I pass, the store is closed. Today it's open but the dress is no longer in the window. When I walk in, it's hanging on a rack next to the cash register with a "sold" ticket pinned to it (in my size too). Heartbroken, I ask if there is another and the shop owner sadly shakes her head no. She does however, have the same one in beige in my size and it fits perfectly. It's the ultimate, Italian designer dress under which only the scantiest panties might be worn...no need for a bra because it has light boning to hold the breasts up perfectly. Looking at my reflection in the mirror, my breasts are front and center, and I doubt I have the guts to wear it in public. I ask the sales woman, *"E bene cosi?"* Is it all right like this? She pushes out her lower lip, shrugs her shoulders up and gestures with open hands, *"Certo*! Why not? You have beautiful breasts," she tells me. "How could it be more perfect?"

I buy it because I adore it and it makes me feel like an Italian movie star. Perhaps I'll never get up the nerve to wear it, but I don't care. Buying things I love and allowing an occasion to present itself is often the way I roll...even if it's only in the bedroom. (One week before leaving, I buy a pair of Italian designer spike heels in beige to go with the dress despite the fact that I know I can never wear them on the cobbled streets of Cagliari). I suspect I'll never have the guts to wear this outfit in San Francisco either, but I take the Scarlet O'Hara approach: I'll worry about that tomorrow.

Following my purchase, I pop into the local grocer's and buy ingredients to recreate a version of California Ranch Dressing that I've begun to dearly miss. Bottled dressings are not readily available here, so I make my own, without the benefit of buttermilk, which is also not available. The recipe turns out well and becomes a staple in my kitchen and a new favorite of my Italian and British friends who've not tasted it before.

* * *

I wear another new, more conservative sheath dress that night to meet Paola for dinner at my favorite restaurant, walking down from the Castello to the Bastione and getting appreciative looks from men all along the way. Marino, the owner, welcomes us to Ristorante San Remy, and asks if we have a reservation. We both say yes but he can't find our names. We quickly realize that I assumed Paola had made the reservation and she thought I had. This makes us all laugh and Marino assures us it's not a problem, then shows us to a cozy table beneath an ancient brick arch. Within a minute, two ice-cold glasses of *prosecco* are set before us and we are very happy. My beef carpaccio arrives with arugula and shaved pecorino cheese drizzled with truffle oil onto which the waitress shaves a generous amount of fresh black truffle. A dish like this is my idea of heaven on a plate, and the fresh sautéed *spiegola* (striped bass) that follows is equally delicious.

An intense American couple sits at a table near us and never stops talking and checking their cell phones. Every few minutes they leave to go outside and smoke. I'm not even sure they've eaten anything and when we leave, they are standing outside smoking. I feel like I'm back in Los Angeles in the old days of cocaine. It is a reminder of the level of stress many Americans accept as a matter of course and a stark contrast to the relaxed lifestyle I have become accustomed to here, *il bel far niente.*

After dinner, we stroll down to Piazza San Giovanni in the warm night air to see a unique event combining live music with live art and hundreds of people have already arrived. The well-known artist Mariano Cello, who lives in Villanova and Bosa, is creating on-the-spot watercolor paintings that are projected onto the face of a small, four-story apartment building as he paints. Four musicians play in four different (apartment) windows of the building and Mariano paints a new image to the music of each song. The four windows are backlit to show the musicians amidst the moving painting and their electronically amplified instruments fill the air. The sound system is amazing, and the whole presentation unlike anything I have ever seen. After a while it begins to remind me of the "light shows" my friends used to mount at the Fillmore East in the '60s using transparent inks between glass slides projected onto a screen at the back of the stage. There is a comical moment when an old woman appears in one of the windows that is supposed to remain blacked out. She pulls the curtain in her kitchen window aside, obviously forgetting she is not supposed to do so, and pokes her head out to see what is going on. Everyone laughs at the unplanned comic relief as she quickly pulls back in and closes the curtain. Afterwards, most of the crowd walks around the corner to Bar Florio to party late into the wee hours. I am so grateful to be living here and taking part in this ever-changing Italian movie every day, that tonight feels like Fellini's 8 ½.

I am not the first person to notice that life has a different pace in Italy. It took some time for my body and brain to adjust but it's interesting to notice that I am now on a similar schedule to the one I had in California. I wake between eight and nine and go to sleep between midnight and one. The difference is that I rest and sometimes nap in the afternoon along with the rest of the country. If you've never traveled to Italy, you may not be aware of the hours they keep: all shops, businesses and public places open between nine and ten in the morning, and then close from one until four or five. Everything shuts down with steel shutters that pull down to conceal the entire store. If you happen to arrive during the hours of closure, the city looks like a ghost town. *Restaurants* that serve lunch and dinner open around noon and close by four then reopen at eight thirty p.m. Most people go out to dinner around nine or ten and it's not unusual to see diners arrive at eleven. *Cafeterias* and *osterias* serve only lunch of lighter fare like Panini, lasagna, cold or hot plates, and salads. *Bars* serve continuously from breakfast through dinner and into the early hours of the morning, offering different foods throughout the day and night, along with coffee, beer, freshly squeezed juice, wine and cocktails. Many bars offer a buffet called *apericena* (before dinner) early in the evening – similar to the American happy hour – that costs seven or eight euro for a cocktail and all you can eat buffet. However, as Italians believe food should accompany all alcohol, bars provide complimentary snacks such as chips, olives, nuts, roasted potatoes or small plates of crostini, at all hours alongside any drink. So, eating and drinking is very inexpensive here unless you dine at a fine restaurant and even then, it costs less than half the price of a moderate U.S. restaurant. Due to the mild, warm evenings, food and drink are primarily served outside, so the entire population drinks and dines *al fresco*. I love it. Every piazza has as many places to eat and drink as the number of tables it can accommodate. Friends table-hop from one to another although service is strictly limited to the tables belonging to a particular place.

As soon as people finish work, the city comes alive with a festive air and it feels like a continual happy hour. There is more socialization on a daily basis than in the U.S. where people rarely congregate outside except for a festival or event. Studies such as *The Blue Zone* and many social anthropologists believe this type of socialization and connection creates a healthier and less stressful life style and ultimately, a longer life. People connect on a daily basis here and it is certainly more fun. Every day, following my nap, I shower and change into something beautiful and sexy for my evening out. Even if I don't have plans to meet anyone, I only have to walk out of my apartment to join the rest of the population who are all out for a *passegiatta,* an evening stroll. If I'm not particularly hungry, I might eat a gelato as I stroll instead of dinner. It is a small, walkable city and I invariably run into folks I know. I love the camaraderie of the city, the historical buildings and ruins everywhere, the different neighborhoods and the ever-present vistas of the sea. There is also literally no crime here, so I never feel uncomfortable walking about at any hour. My body loves all the walking too, and my legs feel stronger than they have since I was a professional dancer. I am extremely happy as well as permanently horny.

How horny am I? Standing in front of the glass display case at the local butcher's I stare at the sausages and think, "Wow! Italian sausages are also twice as big as the ones at home. Isn't that amazing?" I am surrounded by a plethora of big dicks. The man behind the counter asks if I know what I want, and I blush deeply and giggle. He smiles and nods as if reading my mind and I point randomly and order two. Do all women traveling in Italy feel like this? I remember hearing someone say that all cities have a character that can be described with one word and that Rome's is sex. Maybe that applies to all of Italy. Or maybe my libido has just been unleashed after my year of celibacy.

On Sardinia, the Italian life style incorporates babies and children of all ages well into the night. When parents go out to socialize with friends or dine in any casual setting, the children go with them. It took a while for me to adjust to five-year old's running around cocktail tables at midnight. Bar Florio and the local pizzerias are always like this, awash with running, screaming children. Parents rarely try to rein them in, and I wonder if the lack of discipline leads to the spoiled nature of Italian men. It may also explain why people here wait until they are in their late thirties or forties to start a family; once you have kids, it's a full-time job.

CHAPTER 4

SINGIN' THE BLUES

———— ◆◆◆◆◆ ————

I was a professional singer and dancer in Broadway musicals in my 20's, and I still love to sing with musicians whenever I can. Few things feel as good as making music with other human beings; it is an indescribable exchange that happens spontaneously in the moment and brings a particular "high" along with it. My heart soars when I hear good, live music and if they play the blues, I often ask to sit in for a song or two because blues are so basic and need no rehearsal. This was on my wish list when I arrived in Sardinia, but I had no idea if Italians would be playing the blues or if they'd be any good. From the moment I arrived, I was surprised to hear American pop music everywhere: in airports, bars, cafes, clothing stores, department store elevators, on buses, etc. Italians are particularly fond of The Eagles, a couple of whom are old friends of mine, so it was particularly funny and heartwarming that their music became the soundtrack of my life in Cagliari! Imagine walking into a seven-hundred-year-old café off a winding street in an ancient *castello*, and hearing "Welcome to the Hotel California."

During my second month in Sardinia, an Italian friend, Sylvia, invites me to join her for "a concert" in her suburban neighborhood. One of the musicians playing is a friend of a friend and she has no idea what kind of music it will be. I was happy to accept and thrilled when it turned out to be jazz. The venue is an elegant nightclub called "B Flat," and as we approach the entrance, a handsome, silver-haired man is greeting and hugging people. "Now, there is an age-appropriate gorgeous man," I think just as Gabriella says, "There's Alessandro." He has a beautiful, big smile and speaks English really well. Within minutes of chatting, Sylvia tells him I'm a singer.

"Do you ever work with vocalists?" I ask.

"Sometimes," he replies.

"Well," I continue, "I'd love to find someone to sing with."

"Maybe I'll call you up tonight," he jokes.

"I'll have to hear you play first," I reply teasingly. In retrospect, I am sorry I didn't say, "Yes, please" instead.

He turns out to be Alessandro di Liberto, an incredible Sardinian jazz musician and an excellent pianist. Introducing the first group of songs, he mentions Sonny Rollins, Charlie Mingus and other names from my New York jazz past, names I haven't heard in conversation for decades. As his quartet begins to play, I remember those long-ago days sitting in Slugs, or the Half Note or Five Spot, the only white person in the audience, transported and vibrating with the feel of the sound coursing through my body. This music does not have the same effect because they "play by the book" (as my pianist mother would say) but Alessandro is wonderful, and I fantasize about singing Billie Holiday songs with him. In the second set, they find their groove.

During the break, I chat with Alessandro at the bar and mention that I'd seen a young talented bass player who I think he would like. He instantly knows who I'm referring to, which is a testament to the small-town vibe of Cagliari. He says, "Mingus is his idol." "Yes," I say. "I told him that Mingus would have been very flattered." When he asks if I ever heard

Mingus play live I tell him about our meeting on the back-stage stairs in Carnegie Hall.

"Are there other jazz clubs in Cagliari?" I ask.

"This one is the best," he says, then mentions two others.

I want to hear him play again, would love to try to sing with him and think he is the handsomest and most charming man I've met thus far. I'm afraid to ask my friends if he's married and assume he is. But I am happy just to know that such a man exists. I know I'll return to B Flat because it's the most elegant club I have visited here (and they also serve Don Julio Reposado).

The following week I try to find Vin Voglio, one of the other clubs Alessandro recommended. It is located in the oldest and highest part of the city called the *Castello,* the former home of the reigning monarchs. I climb all the way up the winding, vertical cobbled streets no wider than the smallest Fiat, but can't find it. A thirty-foot tall, green and blue neon flashing sign on the side of a building reads "*Agenzia la pace"* and I think that might be it but there is no club in sight.

A month later, Lili helps me find the mystery club, Vin Voglio, which I had passed many times without seeing as it was always shuttered during the day. On our way we pass the flashing neon sign I had seen earlier, and she doubles over with laughter, explaining that the sign says, "funeral home." "Does that look like a sign for a funeral home?" I ask her. No, it does not.

A small handwritten sign on the door of Vin Voglio announces that "Black Victor" will be playing the blues that night and I think I jumped up and down in excitement. Later that night, we make our way back to the tiny club at ten p.m. and take seats at the four-seat bar.

"Black Victor" is in fact a white Sardinian, but if you closed your eyes while he sang, you would swear he was African American from the Deep South. He is incredible. Even more incredible is the fact that during the break we discover he speaks no English. This is my first experience of hearing an Italian sing flawlessly in English who is unable to speak the language at all. Lili tells Victor, in Italian, that I am an American blues singer and he invites me to sit in for the next set. I sing a classic twelve bar blues and Victor nails it! He loves my singing and I love his playing, so I sing another one and afterwards, he invites me to sing with him anytime, anywhere. It feels thrilling to sing in a club with a phenomenally gifted musician and I vow to do more whenever I can. Since leaving the musical stage four decades earlier, performances like this are rare and always spontaneous. Now, I feel a need to make them a priority, and to find a way to sing on a more regular basis.

The following October, when I move into the apartment I'll occupy for the next eight months, Vin Voglio is only three blocks away and becomes my local hangout. In fact, it is the only club of any kind in the *castello*. One night, a young British blues singer knocks my socks off playing Mississippi Delta blues and I hear some good jazz there as well. It is an intimate hole-in-the-wall club with only eight small tables and decent wine, and I would have happily spent a lot more evenings there if the young owner had not begun to message me in the wee hours of the morning. We had some innocent flirtatious verbal exchanges but had never so much as touched or kissed. What was he thinking? The night at the bar he asked for my number he said, "Is it ok if I call you sometime?"

"Sure," I said, thinking he meant to call me for a date. Apparently, I'd missed his actual meaning and later that night, when my phone beeped at three a.m., I was surprised to see his name with the question, "Do you sleep?" Yes, actually I had been sleeping and was startled by the late beep, so I checked to be sure it was not an emergency of some kind. The following week, he sent a message at two a.m. asking in English, "I can come?" Not anywhere near me, I thought, and stopped going to his club.

Another similar incident occurred within the same time period that made me wonder: do Italian men think American women have continual sex with random strangers, are Italian women not open to casual sex, were all men psychically able to detect my horniness, or was I sending out the wrong signals? The single Italian men and women I was getting to know did not appear to be very sexually active in fact, many appeared celibate. People socialized in groups of friends where none paired off. In fact, the only people I knew who were having sex were Vittorio, my American friend Christina and my Mexican friend Felicia. This was something I would need to pay more attention to in order to understand. The sexy vibe permeated everything here but how much sex were people really having?

* * *

The following week I sang again when twelve of us ventured out to a club on the outskirts of town. Every Tuesday night in June a band called Non Soul Funky plays and some of my Italian friends love them and invite me to go. My Mexican friend Felicia recommends the gigantic mojitos, and we all start drinking. We are seated at a long table just below the stage and during dinner, an older gentleman approaches and asks if anyone sings. A few of the girls point to me so he asks what I sing. "Blues, torch songs, standards, rock'n'roll," I list, to which he responds, "Ok, blues," and then walks away. I wondered if he is drunk or just trying to make conversation with a group of women and I think no more about it.

A while later, the band starts to play, and they are great; singing in perfect English and we all enjoy it. Then, the lead vocalist says something in Italian, followed by my name and all the Italians at our table began to clap and say *vai* ("go") to me.

"Where?" I asked my friends.

"They are asking you to go up and sing with them," they explain.

"But what am I supposed to sing?"

"You tell them," they say.

I had drunk a giant mojito and two glasses of wine, so this sounded fine. The lead singer speaks to me in rapid Italian as I climb up onto the stage and when he sees I do not understand asks, "What you sing?"

"Blues," I reply.

"Blues," he calls to the keyboard player.

My heart sinks. This is not going to work. After quickly assessing the situation, I walk to the piano player and ask in English, "Do you know any blues songs?"

"Blues?" he repeats and begins playing a standard riff.

"OK," I say, "can you play that in G?"

"Blues in G?" he repeats.

"Si," I say nodding my head yes. "Blues in G."

Meanwhile the lead singer is still talking in rapid Italian to the audience and clowning around about "blues" while the keyboard player riffs in my key. Unsure what to do, I hold my hand up and say loudly "*Aspetta!*" (stop) and everyone stops. I walk to the lead singer and smile as I take the mic from him and sing a long, loud, soulful "oh yeahhhh." The singer's jaw drops. He says, "wow!" bows to me and leaves the stage.

I sing *Stormy Monday* to hoots and hollers from the audience and the band follows seamlessly. A few of my friends' video the performance on their phones from the moment I take the stage and it is great to watch the entire interaction that might easily have gone completely sour. Instead it is a triumph over language and cultural barriers; proof that music truly transcends both – and I even enjoy hearing myself sing on the video, which is unusual for me. A few months later, I would sing with them again in the fabulous B Flat nightclub. I wish I could accurately describe the feeling that results from a live performance, but it is unlike anything else; a spontaneous interaction between vocalist and musicians that can never be exactly repeated. Each participant is responsible for making the sounds that belong only to him/her simultaneously with the others. When it works, it is nothing short of magical and to achieve that without rehearsal is its own special magic. I don't think I realized how much I missed that until I experienced it again.

Six months into my year in Italy, I discover Jazzino, a small elegant supper club that offers live music and a fixed price five-course menu with wine for twenty-five euro. It is small and elegant, serves some of the best nouvelle cuisine in Cagliari and the owner is a former sound engineer who installed an ideal sound system. Jazzino becomes my favorite hangout because of the diverse musical performances in an intimate setting with great food. Black Victor played there and when he saw me in the audience, invited me to sing with him. On another occasion, I sat in with a "by-the-book" blues band that was less than inspirational. By the end of my year abroad I had sung with five bands in six venues in three countries, which my daughter would later dub my "European tour."

CHAPTER 5

SUMMER EXODUS

$\diamond\!\diamond\!\blacklozenge\!\diamond\!\diamond$

July continues to swelter and all I want is a dip in the sea. For the last month, as soon as my school day ends, I hop on a bus on Via Roma and head out to Poetto Beach with the rest of the citizens of Cagliari. The beach is expansively wide and many miles long, so it never feels crowded. Small identical structures called "kiosks" sit at the back of the beach every few hundred feet and they offer comfortable canvas-slung beach chairs and light fare along with coffee, wine, beer and cocktails. The bus stops near our favorite one and without making plans, I often find many of my friends there. The sea is warm, clear, shallow and waveless, making it easy to dip in and out and stay refreshed. One day, Lili met me for a snack after school and said she needed cheering up. "I just bought a new pair of mirrored sun glasses. Can we go to Poetto to look at beautiful Italian dick in speedos?" she asked in her lovely British accent. So, I was not the only one to notice. We did that a lot and the men seemed to enjoy seeing us in our bikinis too.

When Tonio finishes work early on Friday, he picks me up and we drive south along the coast to the famous beach, Mari Pintou (painted beach). As we round a sharp curve high above the sea, I catch my first glimpse of a small post-card-perfect cove with breathtaking turquoise water. The beach is covered with round, smooth, white stones instead of sand but the water has a soft white sandy bottom. (Wouldn't Sandy Bottom be a great name for a drag queen?) A concession sells drinks and snacks and rents beautiful beach chairs with built-in sunshades, and there are only about thirty other people on the beach.

From the comfort of our sling chairs, we watch some big, gorgeous yachts pass by and a sleek sailboat – like the one in the Lina Wertmuller film *Swept Away* – anchors offshore to give passengers time to swim. For a brief moment, I imagine myself living that life instead of this one and decide that this one is just fine for now. I have decided to allow my skin to tan for the first time in thirty years and it's already turning a light golden brown. If the Italians could why couldn't I? When in Rome, right? Perhaps, Italian sunshine isn't damaging to the skin.

We spend a lovely, relaxing afternoon swimming and lolling in the turquoise sea and when I get home my daughter, Ariane, Face Times me around ten p.m. to ask if I've heard the big news from America. Amazingly, I have. It is only the second news I've heard from America in two months, the first being the slaughter of nine innocent black people in a Charleston church. This afternoon, when Tonio was turning off the Internet on his phone he read aloud, "U.S. Supreme Court passes the equal rights marriage act." So, my daughter – a long-time supporter of sexual equality – and most of northern California is celebrating. Once again, I wish Malone were here to see this and remember the summer night in 1969 when he came running into our West Greenwich Village apartment breathless and disheveled to tell me the police had just raided the Stonewall (a popular gay nightclub) and he and his friends had fought them! This event entered history as "the Stonewall Riots" and signaled the birth of the gay rights movement whose chant became, "We're here, we're queer, get used to it!" My throat constricts, and eyes fill with tears at the memory but then in typical Malone style, I hear him say, "Of course we should have equal rights but why would I ever want to get married when I can have all the men I want? No thank you." In those days of our early twenties, we were too busy being free spirits to want real intimacy. I suddenly realize he'd died before having a chance to grow up and experience a real loving relationship; the very thing I miss so much right now. Then it strikes me as ironic that he was my most intimate partner though our relationship never included sex. I still feel his loss deeply after more than twenty-five years and suppose I always will.

Later that night, at eleven forty-five, I am sitting at the kitchen table writing, when Tonio calls to ask if I want to go to "an outside space" to tango. Ten minutes later, he picks me up and we drive to an area with a long, covered marble walkway between two modern office buildings. The evening is hot and balmy, I imagine like Buenos Aires. He sets up his music and speakers and we dance for an hour in the gentle evening air. It feels incredibly romantic and unlike any other moment in my life. Once again, I feel like I am in a movie because things like this don't happen in real life. My young lover and I are dancing tango outside all alone on a marble surface in the middle of the night, in the middle of an ancient city. It is magical! Throughout the summer, a weekly tango *milonga* is held on Friday nights in Cagliari. Hundreds of dancers gather opposite the marina in a huge marble plaza off Via Roma. The music fills the air and it is the most romantic and beautiful tango evening I have ever seen. As I feel the essence of the dance begin to settle into my body, I hope to dance at that *milonga* before I leave next summer.

Afterward we go to Florio for a spritz and the piazza is packed with people. Lili is there and, miraculously, they have a brand-new bottle of Espolon Reposado. I am very, very happy but only stay for one. Tonio walks me home and as we kiss, I think, "I'm going to need to teach him how to kiss."

When I first met Tonio, he told me he was very "tactile." Californians would label him "touchy-feely." In fact, he really just enjoyed feeling himself up. It was a habit I found repulsive; running one of his hands underneath his shirt and up his chest to caress himself in public, in restaurants. It was the first red flag. He was a very smart, left-brained scientist, who had taken a course in massage therapy and enjoyed "practicing" on me. This was how we actually connected physically for the first time; a ten-minute massage that turned into an hour of sex. It was slow and sensual and quite enjoyable but afterward, I cried. Since this had also happened with Vittorio I wasn't surprised. A year without sex had passed prior to my tryst with Vittorio and I assumed my tears were a reaction to being intimate with someone other than Luke. When it happened a fourth and fifth time, I had to examine the possibility that something else was going on and that "something else" turned out to be that sex without love depressed me. I was spoiled by six years of passionate sex combined with deep love, and now sex by itself felt empty. Tonio's sensuality helped to soothe that but it was still, ultimately, unfulfilling.

I think about this for a few days and decide to try an experiment to help me embrace sex on its own. Accomplishing this might require role-play; doing something out of character for me. Did I need to be more selfish or to take control? I ask myself what might make me feel better and the answer is easy: an orgasm. Tonio had called earlier to say he was running late and then didn't show up at the later time. It was not the first time he had done this. Angered and annoyed by this lack of respect, I wanted to teach him a lesson so, I chose a role he had never seen me in and was ready by the time he arrived. I open the door wearing a smile, a red lace demi bra, red lace thong, and red fuck me pumps. When he tries to caress my ass, I smack his hand away and say, "I didn't say you could touch me." Then I saunter slowly down the hall toward the bedroom and say sweetly over my shoulder, "You can come in here."

He follows me into the bedroom, and I say, "You were late and disrespectful, and all women deserve respect so, undress then lie on the couch." He follows my directions, clearly both uncomfortable and intrigued. By the time he removes his underwear he is fully erect. I smile at the display, and then gently push him onto his back. I say. "This is what happens when you're late."

I straddle his face, pulling my thong aside and opening myself so he can lick me. I do not change positions until achieving a full and satisfying orgasm, and then I slide down the length of his body and put him inside me. It is the best sex we ever have and the first time I don't miss good kisses. There are no tears afterwards either. In that moment, I give up wanting him to be something other than he is. This man would never take Luke's place or be anything more than a sex and dance partner. It felt good to put him in that place and my sadness around him not being what I want instantly dissipates.

However, the realization that I am still in love with Luke upsets me on many levels. I had put an ocean between us and taken two lovers almost half my age. Shouldn't that add up to "I'm all right now?" Shouldn't I be having a good time? In fact, I am not. The more sex I have with Tonio, the more I get to know him, the less I like him. I do not enjoy kissing him and for me, kissing is one of the most intimate aspects of sex. He is addicted to drama and I have carefully opted for a "drama-free" life since divorcing my last husband. I realize that the only time I really enjoy being with him is when we're dancing tango. Dancing feels like the only time Tonio is capable of intimacy with me. Perhaps, the dance has become a substitute kind of intimacy for him and he no longer needs another.

Tonio also shares the irritating qualities of many Italian men who continue to depend on their mothers into adulthood for food, financial assistance and approval. He eats lunch at his mother's house every day and leaves with containers of food for his dinner. An opportunity to move to a big city on the mainland presented itself but he would not take it without his mother's consent. I think he also does not want to forgo the free, prepared food supply. Did I mention he was forty-one years old? Why do these women keep the apron strings pulled so tightly and why do Italian men have such a difficult time growing up? I try to think of any American man I've been with who relied on his mother for anything more than an occasional home cooked meal, past the age of twenty and cannot.

When I realize Tonio has become annoying to me, I know the end is near. Things start to formally unwind during a weekend jazz festival. I had purchased two tickets to the three-day event earlier in the spring, thinking I'd invite a friend. It was in *Parco Dei Suoni,* (park of sounds) a former stone quarry that had been converted into a unique outdoor venue for music. Arranged over several acres, it incorporated the natural remnants of the quarry walls to define and separate three different stages without noise pollution from one stage to another, making it possible for three bands to play at one time. When I decided to invite Tonio, I went online to see if I could find an interesting hotel nearby and was excited to find a *terme*, natural hot spring spa and hotel. It was a bit pricey, so we decided to stay just one night and attend the festival for two days. In retrospect, this was a fortunate decision.

We drive about two hours on a Saturday morning, stopping to see a few sights along the way, and arrive at the hotel in time for a late lunch. The hotel has seen better days, but I am happy to be out of the city and it feels relaxing, despite the pool of screaming children. The mineral water pools turn out to be a big disappointment as they are heavily chlorinated. I fail to understand the theory behind soaking in chlorinated water and can only remain submerged for ten minutes before the fumes begin to burn my eyes. So much for the healing water idea.

Outside the familiarity of the city, Tonio becomes more comfortable with me, revealing more about himself. However, the more he reveals, the more turned off I become. He is obsessively in love with a woman who has made it clear she has no interest in him whatsoever. For some delusional reason, he believes she will change her mind. This unrequited love has been going on for more than a year, and whenever I ask the simple question, "How are you doing?" he replies, "I am suffering." Seriously?

"Why do you want to suffer?" I ask.

To which he replies, "It is not my choice."

"Really? Whose choice is it?"

In my world, how we react is always our choice and his response tells me a lot about him, primarily that he is immature. In California, we would call him unconscious. As a person who has spent her entire adult life intrigued by and actively seeking to become more self-aware, I find this tiresome.

When I share my feelings on this subject I quickly understand that he is in fact, *committed* to suffering. He believes it to be admirable or noble with some romanticized notion that equates suffering with loving deeply at any cost. This propensity shows up in other relationships as well with his job, ex-girlfriend and family. I explain that telling an American you are "suffering" is not in any way appealing, nor is it likely to elicit a compassionate response. It just sounds pathetic. Some of my friends back home might refer to this as "a negative vibration." For me, it is simply the ultimate turn-off.

Tonio had also been unresponsive to my requests for softer deeper kisses and persisted in sucking on my lips until they were bruised. After the third ugly purple bruise appeared on my upper lip, I stopped kissing him. There was also the matter of his ex-girlfriend, who he insisted I meet – this mythically youthful "older woman" (quite a few years younger than me) of whom he spoke so highly.

When we were finally introduced, I hope my face did not reveal my shock. At fifty-nine years old, she looked like a dowdy seventy-year-old, with a plump matronly body and badly dyed orange hair. Seeing them together, one would naturally assume they were mother and son. It made me take a hard look at myself in the mirror and question the wisdom in taking young lovers. Like his relationship with his mother, he was still attached to his ex-lover's apron strings, meeting for coffee regularly, talking on the phone multiple times a day, picking her up and dropping her off, etc. He had found another mother. Dear God, was I to be a third? After two years of separation, his ex still had no idea he saw other women. "She needs me," he explained. "Just like your mother does," I thought.

* * *

All of these things add up to an ending for me, and I tell him this as gently as I can on our way home from the jazz fest. He is shocked! After much discussion, I repeat that I still hope to dance tango with him, and he agrees. And then, to completely discourage him from any thoughts of continuing, I tell him my age and that I've been married five times. I want to be certain it is over.

* * *

By the second week in July, I am free of lovers and the city of Cagliari has become an unbearable steam bath. Without air conditioning, my apartment is so hot by the time I arrive home from school at three, all I can do is shower the sweat off my body, strip naked, turn on the portable fan and hope to fall asleep for a couple of hours. It is too hot to remain in my apartment to study at night, so I pass the evenings like everyone else in Cagliari, in outdoor cafes or Bar Florio, grateful for the mediocre tequila. Many of these hot summer nights are spent with Lili, who is delightful and shares the same sense of humor, a gift in a foreign country. Often, we laugh ourselves silly and she serves as my interpreter for Italian when conversations go too fast.

On one such evening, we are joined by a group of six young Italian men Lili knows from the school where she teaches English. When I say young, I mean mid-twenties. She and I have been drinking tequila for a while when one of the boys lights up a pot-laced cigarette and passes it around. It is the first pot I've smoked (or even seen) in four months, and despite the harshness of the tobacco, it makes me instantly giddy. The eight of us are sitting outside Florio around a table and only one of the boys speaks a little English. Lili, sitting on my left, moves her eyes around the group, resting them on one boy at a time, to give me a brief description. On the far side of the table, the most beautiful one has been gazing intently at his cell phone deep in concentration for several minutes. Lili regards him and then says quietly to me, in a very serious tone, "He's choosing an emoticon." We don't stop laughing for a good five minutes.

By the third week in July, the heat and humidity are unbearable, and I understand why Italians flee their cities in summer. The final blow is delivered when my landlord informs me that two Russian students have specifically reserved my room and will be arriving in five days. No explanation is offered as to why she would agree to rent a room that has already been rented for three months and she offers to move me into one of the dreaded back rooms. The apartment still has no Internet, no functional washing machine, no air conditioning and no screens on the windows or doors. Classes in the school are filling up with young foreign students coming and going every week. It suddenly seems like the perfect time to travel, and I decide to leave the apartment and Cagliari for the rest of the summer.

Now that I know the city better, it will be easy to find a new apartment when I return. It feels wonderful to have the freedom to do this and I am suddenly excited.

CHAPTER 6
ALGHERO, ATHENS AND IKARIA

M y "escape the city" plan is provided by an old friend and neighbor who had recently contacted me out of the blue. I had known David Kahn in the early '70s on Malibu Beach; now he and his wife, Robyn, lived in Greece and graciously extended an invitation to visit them on the tiny island of Ikaria. This little piece of paradise happens to be one of five locations made famous by the book *Blue Zones*, where it is common for people to live active, healthy lives well past one hundred years of age! Serendipitously, David and Robyn run a travel business specific to Greece and Turkey. "Wow!" I say to David, "Could you help me with a trip to Istanbul?" "Of course," he laughs and then adds the fact that his partner for the Turkish end of the business happens to be the niece of the last Sultan of the Ottoman Empire. I am stunned speechless to learn this as I had spent the previous twenty years writing two historical novels about the Ottoman Sultans from whom she had descended. I am so excited I can hardly contain myself. Not only will I get to meet Nilgun Sirin, the direct descendant of the last Sultan, she will arrange private tours, with historians as guides, to show me all the places I had written about and never seen!

Within forty-eight hours of speaking with David, I have mapped out my travel plans. I will spend two weeks in the seaside city of Alghero, to see the northern end of Sardinia and fly direct from there to Athens to spend one night and then catch an early morning puddle jumper to Ikaria. Only one daily flight operates from Athens to the island, and David warned they booked up months in advance. Magically, I find one seat on the exact day I need. While on Ikaria, David and Robyn will help me to arrange my trip to Turkey with Nilgun. This is an unexpected gift, and an opportunity I could never have imagined.

Remember the wish list I made before I left on this trip?

1. Live in Sardinia and travel around Italy.
2. Learn to speak Italian.
3. Learn Argentine tango.
4. Sing (blues) with foreign bands.
5. Visit some Greek islands.
6. Visit the sites where my historical novels took place in Istanbul.
7. Sail to small Turkish and Greek islands and visit Ephesus on a traditional Turkish *goulette* (wooden sailboat).

I have already checked off the first four wishes and will now embark on a trip, hopefully to check off the rest.

The first leg of my trip becomes more interesting when Lili introduces me (through email) to her friend Helen, a Brit who lives in Alghero. Lili describes her as "one of the funniest and most interesting people I know if half the stories she tells are true." Turns out she is, and they are.

During the first two days of my stay, Helen and I are unable to connect, so I explore the city on my own. Alghero is a gorgeous resort with an interesting old walled city directly on the sea. A graciously wide pedestrian walkway atop the ancient retaining wall encircles the part of the city facing the sea for several kilometers. Side-by-side restaurants line this wall for outside dining with spectacular views and people stroll there day and night. The restaurants are more upscale than those in Cagliari, and I find the food more interesting with a lot more seafood.

The nights are warm and balmy, without Cagliari's humidity, and I stay out late with everyone else, dining, strolling, sipping mojitos and eating gelato. As I walk along the ramparts of the former fort, a "blood moon" is setting; a moon that's actually red as the name implies and eerily beautiful. I watch it slip into the sea too fast, not wanting it to go. As it disappears a deep sadness creeps into my bones and I think (rather poetically): I am a writer, a singer and a dancer. I am also a woman of uncertain age studying the Italian language and tango. I am a lover and a dreamer, living my dream and that of many others. If I am doing the right thing, why does it sometimes feel so wrong?

* * *

The next night, I take my host's suggestion and walk down to a sidewalk bar along the yacht harbor called *Marecaraibo* (Caribbean Sea) where nostalgic American music by my old friends, The Eagles, still follows me. I sip a Campari spritz on the waterfront as the sun sets and *Tequila Sunrise* begins to play. It makes my heart heavy, and I wish I wasn't alone in this moment. I begin to slide down the familiar, uncomfortable slope of doubt and loneliness and write the following poem:

Put away the moon
Put away the sea
Put away the memory of how we used to be
It hurts too much to think about
But now and then I try
To see if it still feels the same
And then, to ponder why.

I finish my drink and walk back to my B&B to fall soundly asleep. The next night I'm drawn back to the beautiful sadness of *Marecaraibo*: it's another sunset, alone on the sea with a Campari spritz. Overhearing the conversation of a young couple next to me, I at first don't recognize the language, only to realize a few minutes later they're speaking English. How long have I been in Italy? Three months. As the light fades, a young bearded man sporting a tiny American flag Speedo begins dancing on the sea wall. It seems he's channeling Malone, and my eyes fill with tears as I hear Malone say, "Pull yourself together, darling. You're still alive and you'll ruin your mascara." Thanks, Malone.

* * *

I'm grateful that Helen and I get together the next day, and she does not disappoint. She's a smart and funny ball of energy, and I adore her instantly! Coincidentally, my B&B is just a block from her apartment, so she introduces me to some locals in the neighborhood. One couple owns a small bar between Helen's place and mine that becomes a favored destination for nightcaps. One night, at about one a.m., the tipsy owner decides to turn on a Karaoke machine. She sings (or more accurately, murders) a couple of songs, at which point Helen reveals I'm a singer. After much translation, searching and writing things down, the husband finds a version of *Desperado*. I'd be lying if I said I didn't enjoy people's reactions to my voice, and since everyone wants me to keep singing, I happily do for a while. It doesn't count as "singing blues with a foreign band in Italy" but it makes me very happy and feels like I am following through with my intention to sing more.

* * *

The next day, as I head toward my B&B, I notice a very handsome man walking towards me. He is tall, with longish sandy hair and green eyes, smiling as I come near. I return the smile and wonder why I can't meet someone like that. Later that evening, as Helen and I walk to her friend's bar for a nightcap, he is there. "That's the guy I saw earlier today," I whisper to Helen. She grabs my arm and pulls me close to whisper in my ear, "That's Paolo, my friend's brother." What extraordinary luck! She introduces us, and we chat and flirt for the rest of the evening but unfortunately, he's leaving to return to his home and business an hour away and I'll be leaving for Greece. Paolo becomes one of the beautiful love stories that never happened.

Helen and I book a day trip on a local boat with twenty other tourists that departs at nine am. As soon as we're under way, the crew of four adorable young Italians serves espressos and answers our questions about the different areas we pass. We sail by huge, white chalk cliffs that drop dramatically into the sea, and an elaborate resort that dominates an entire hillside. We motor out for over an hour to a small turquoise cove with a tiny beach that is unfortunately already occupied by a big family with full camping gear: a tarp shade shelter, chairs, tables, coolers, a hibachi grill and half a dozen children. Four teenagers repeatedly scale the rocky cliff next to the beach to jump off the highest point into the sea and I watch them enviously, wishing I had grown up in such a place.

When the crew asks if anyone wants to swim almost everyone says yes and within minutes, a Zodiac appears off our boat, dropping huge inflated rafts into the sea. Helen and I strip down to the swimsuits under our shorts, and dive into the clear water. It's divine. From the water, we look back at our boat to see a family of four being loaded onto the Zodiac. They happen to be a particularly unattractive family who are, in fact, so miserable that Helen and I had commented to each other about it earlier. They've seemed unhappy since the trip began.

We float around for another ten minutes, when the Zodiac reappears carrying four bikini-clad young women. Where did they find these beautiful girls? And where did they take the family?

A little while later, we all climb back into the boat while the crew fits a nifty grilling apparatus onto the bow to cook meat, fish and vegetables. By the time lunch is ready we're all ravenous. Our delicious meal is followed by strong Italian espresso and most of us get back in the water to snooze aboard the big rafts. It's a perfect day that costs about forty euro and we never discover how the passenger exchange had been made.

After ten days in Alghero, I am excited to depart for Greece but sad to leave my fabulous new friend, Helen. I have not seen David and Robyn for over twenty years and a surprise awaits me in Athens that I could never have imagined.

On July 22, I take a direct flight to Athens where I've booked a hotel near the airport to make my early morning flight to Ikaria the following day. The hotel has booked a private car for me in lieu of a taxi, saying it would cost the same and be more reliable. They tell me the driver will be waiting outside customs holding a sign with my name.

As the automatic doors open from customs to the waiting area, I see a jostling crowd of about one hundred people, behind which drivers stand in a row, holding signs. I make my way through the crowd and begin walking down the long row of drivers looking for my name. Rolling my suitcase past twenty grizzled older men, I finally spot my name and break into a wide grin. The young man holding the sign is gorgeous! "Thank you," I say silently to the universe, "for this beautiful gift." When he sees that I recognize my name, he also starts grinning and asks with open surprise, "Zia Wesley?"

"Yes, I am," I reply.

He reaches for everything I'm carrying, shouldering my heavy bag, and taking the handle to my rolling suitcase.

"My name Nikos," he says, placing his hand on his chest. "I can call you Zia?"

"Yes, please," I say, thinking: you can call me anything your little heart desires.

"Car is outside," he continues with a grin. "We go out now, please."

He's six feet tall, with the body of an athlete, dark sparkling eyes, dimples, and a gorgeous smile. His short, dark hair is perfectly groomed and spikey in the front, very hip. He wears a crisp red and white-checkered shirt with the sleeves rolled twice and faded, tight jeans. I will later learn he is, in fact, an ex-pro soccer player.

On our short walk to the car, he uses the little English he knows to ask if my flight was ok, if I was traveling alone and if I was married. Wow, I think, Greek men don't waste any time. When we reach the car, he invites me to sit up front, but I'm too flustered and choose the back. He says, "Zia, you are very beautiful. Why you are alone?" I laugh and say it's complicated. He looks at me in the rear-view mirror or over his shoulder for the entire drive and we speak as much as our language differences will allow for the thirty-minute trip.

Before arriving at the hotel, he asks if I wish to go out for something to eat or to hear some music. Were I not so travel-weary, I might be inclined to accept the offer. But all I want is to fall into bed and sleep, knowing I have to get up to an alarm much earlier than usual the next morning. So, I decline, and he says he'll see me in the morning when he picks me up to take me back to the airport.

The next morning, he arrives wearing a very expensive and beautifully pressed shirt, with sleeves rolled further past his elbows to show off his tan muscled arms, and even tighter, ripped and faded jeans that hug the perfectly formed muscles of his thighs. He looks good enough to eat with a spoon and I kick myself for not taking him up on his offer the previous night. When he opens the door on the front passenger side, I gladly slide onto the front seat. He smiles and opens the conversation with, "Zia, why you are not married?"

"I'm divorced," I say. "Are you married?"

"Yes," he says, "And two children I love very much."

"And you only proposition American women who are passing through?" I want to ask. Instead, I say, "Does your wife know you go out with foreign women?"

"No!" he protests, "I not go with other woman, I good boy but you so beautiful."

I laugh and say, "Oh, it's only me. Of course."

"Only you," he repeats with a sad smile. Oh god, he's so adorable I feel like Shirley Valentine.

"Well," I tell him, "I might fly through Athens again on my way home in the next couple months. Can I call you to pick me up if I do?"

"Yes, for sure!" he says, giving me his business card and adding his email. He asks if I'm on Facebook and when I say yes, he says to friend him—but adds that he and his wife share the account so...I understand. He hugs me goodbye at the airport, then holds my arms and looks deeply into my eyes to say he hopes to see me again. I don't want him to remove his hands and for the briefest moment I consider postponing my flight for a day.

The flight to Ikaria takes only an hour, and I'm sure I smile the whole way. The tiny airport is on the island's dry west side and not especially picturesque. As I disembark I see a tall man leaning against a fence post and as soon as he sees me he shakes his head. It has been over twenty years since we last saw each other, and his first words are, "How do you do it? You look exactly the same."

"So, do you," I reply, and it's true. David has a bit less hair but retains the swimmer's physique and beautiful smile. His lovely wife, Robyn, is waiting nearby and greets me warmly. They apologize for the funky car, which is impossible to keep clean on the island's dusty, unpaved roads and I assure them I could not care less.

As we drive, they tell me about the island they've called home for the past twenty-five years, explaining that the airport is on the opposite side from where they live, about an hour and a half away. The plan is to stop in a little seaside village along the way for lunch.

The topography begins to change to lush green within thirty minutes of driving, and by the time we reach our lunch destination, there is a profusion of flowers everywhere: purple, orange and yellow wild flowers, fuchsia bougainvilleas climbing over walls and houses, and pots of flowers in window boxes on every window. The town is tiny, with neat white stucco houses climbing up the hills surrounding the little port where two restaurants offer outside seating. David, who is fluent in Greek, orders for us and everything they bring is delicious; fresh, local and flavorful. One of the dishes, *horta*, resembles sautéed spinach, but David explains that it is in fact, boiled wild weeds prepared with olive oil and lemon. He explains that it is a popular local dish made from whatever weeds the cook gathers on his way to work! I love this idea and it becomes one of my favorite dishes for the rest of my stay. Over the next month, Robyn helps me identify some of the two hundred different varieties of edible weeds that grow everywhere, and we cook them up for meals at her house. They also have a lovely and prolific vegetable garden that provides all of the fresh ingredients we cook and eat…something I dearly miss living in an Italian city.

After lunch we drive the rest of the way to Arministis, the town where I'll be staying in a little hotel overlooking gorgeous Livadi Beach. The hotel is a white stucco building with bright blue trim. Stone paths lead along the cliff from the rooms to the outdoor dining patio that also overlooks the sea. It's picture-perfect (and very inexpensive) with steep stone stairs leading down to the wide, wave less beach where the water gently laps at the shore. I never knew that unlike oceans, seas only have waves in storms, and this is why the water is crystal clear. On the beach below the hotel, a big wooden shack-like structure with a thatched palm roof serves drinks and food and rents beach chairs for two euro a day. David settles me into my lovely room with a private patio facing the sea and a big window with wooden shutters opening onto the patio. He explains that their house is a ten-minute drive straight up the mountain and they'll pick me up for dinner around eight. I open the shutters wide to let in the warm floral scented sea air and could not be happier.

The island of Ikaria is about as untouched by the modern world as any place I have ever been. There are no wide highways or well-paved roads, no cities or shopping centers, no chain stores, super markets or fast food restaurants; only small locally owned businesses, many of which are only open in the summer. Very few people have televisions and Internet and cell service is limited to certain areas. There are about two hundred fifty very small towns where generations of families have lived for thousands of years. Through millennia, the island has survived invasions by pirates, Romans, Moors, Spaniards, Turks, and Nazis. It has never been "invaded" by the discothèque-loving Europeans who have turned Mykonos and other islands into my version of tourist hell. Ikaria is one of the loveliest, unspoiled places I have ever been and will most likely remain so because there is "nothing to do" there. In short, a perfect place for a writer.

Spending five weeks on Ikaria with its incredibly slow pace of daily life, brought me to a rare deep state of peace and relaxation. It was like an extended silent meditation retreat but with great conversations, cocktails and dancing. The time enabled me to quietly delve into some of the emotions around my separation from love and family and to begin to explore my feelings about my new solitary state. Being around David and Robyn and witnessing their relationship of twenty-five years gave me hope of finding one of my own. They were both independent and accomplished and had found a way to live very remotely on a tiny foreign island in the middle of the sea; that in itself was a huge accomplishment. It was country living in an old stone house they had slowly remodeled with fruit and olive trees, the big vegetable garden and a steep dirt road about a quarter mile walk to the town below. I could picture myself there but not alone.

However, throughout the months of July and August, every one of the two hundred fifty towns on the island hosts a non-stop party called a Panigiri, in celebration of their patron saint. In preparation for these events, the road leading to the town is blocked off and the town square is lined on all sides with long tables and benches; enough to accommodate hundreds of people. A stage is erected at one end of the square and one of the town's buildings is converted to a makeshift cafeteria to serve the roasted pork, goat and lamb dinner. It's extraordinarily well organized by the townspeople volunteering to serve and prep. The cost for dinner, with wine, is twenty-five euro and includes potatoes, salad, yogurt dressing, bread and water. Wine is also available but undrinkable to me. David says it's "an acquired taste," but in my six weeks there, I never acquire that particular taste. I do drink the incredibly strong turpentine-like Raki, which may have taken some of the enamel off my teeth.

At eight p.m. a band of twelve Greek musicians begins to play and does not stop until eight a.m. When one of the musicians needs a break, another takes his place. Four generations of families gather for these events and typically, everyone dances until dawn. And everyone knows the steps of each dance; hands are held to form one long chain that snakes into concentric circles and if someone like myself is unsure of the steps, the people on either side silently demonstrate and gently correct. Never in my life have I experienced anything like this. The only event that comes close is a big Italian wedding but that would only last five to eight hours at the most and the only dance that everyone does together is the Tarantella!

I had the good fortune to attend four Panigiri during the five weeks I spent on Ikaria and think they are the best parties I ever attended. Dancing alongside great-grandmothers dancing with their sons, daughters, grandchildren and great grandchildren is indescribable. I am so grateful to Robyn for teaching me some of the dances beforehand and think I only sat down to eat. The only downside occurred when David, Robyn and I left the Panigiri in the town below their house at four a.m. and were unable to sleep because the loud music sounded like it was right outside our windows...even with earplugs... for the next four hours.

One day, Robyn takes me on a most unusual excursion to a natural *terme* (hot spring) that bubbles up into the Ionian Sea. We drive an hour to the west side of the island, park on the side of the road and climb down a steep cliff. It takes about twenty minutes to cross a beach covered entirely with huge boulders we have to climb over, to reach our point of entry into the sea; it is a moss-covered boulder we first climb up and then slide down into the boiling hot sea! Robyn's instructions are to "move out of the super-hot water as fast as you can." The whole approach is dicey but worth it. It feels strange to float in the buoyant salt water that is both hot and cold. The naturally protected pool is about fifty by one hundred feet and only four feet deep with hot spouts that bubble up between our legs through the pebbled bottom. The other interesting caveat is that the water is "radioactive," and we can only stay in safely for twenty minutes. We emerge utterly stoned. I sit on the boulders in meditation for over an hour afterwards, and neither of us remembers anything about the long drive home, after which we both fall sound asleep for several hours. It is a unique experience and I feel so grateful to have shared it with Robyn. I realize that Ikaria is simultaneously inspiring and depressing; an example of what I long for and do not have. Over the years I have lived in remote areas in North Carolina, Upstate New York, and Colorado but always with a partner. When I try to imagine where I prefer to live in the coming years, I picture a setting much like David and Robyn's but for would not want to be alone there. I can picture myself living alone in some type of suburban community or small town where I could walk to town from my house for socialization and shopping but going home to an empty house feels lonely and a "home nest" is very important for me. I love to cook for people and enjoy sharing those meals with people I love. Imagining a future alone does not give me a warm fuzzy feeling even if it means travel. I keep thinking that something unexpected will reveal itself and maintain hope that it does. But what if it doesn't? I need a backup plan but so far none exists.

* * *

During my second week on Ikaria, David and I call Nilgun and begin to plan my trip to Istanbul. I ask about the *goulette* and she says she will investigate for me. A couple of weeks later, everything except the *goulette* has been planned. Nilgun arranges for guides to be with me throughout my ten day stay in Istanbul, after which I will fly to Izmir on the West coast and be driven from there to the seaside resort of Kusadasi where I'll stay in the hotel belonging to her cousins, the grandchildren of the last Sultan of Turkey! She has also arranged a guide to accompany me on a full day trip to visit the ancient city of Ephesus a ninety-minute drive from Kusadasi. Miraculously, I will be checking all my wishes off my list!

* * *

I was excited to see big, healthy cilantro plants growing in David and Robyn's garden because cilantro did not exist on Sardinia. I found a tiny bunch once in a "foreign gourmet" grocers there and promptly made salsa but there was not enough to make my favorite cilantro salad dressing that I love, and I was excited to be able to share that recipe with these dear friends. We cooked delicious meals together many nights from their beautiful garden and David was happy to have me cook some of his old Mexican favorites...the dishes he used to eat in local restaurants in Malibu that he never learned to make. I loved watching him enthusiastically devour roasted chicken smothered in pico de gallo and cold roasted garden vegetable salad with cilantro dressing. They grew several varieties of peppers in their garden and I taught Robyn how to make rajas, the classic sautéed Mexican accompaniment to many dishes. It felt wonderful to be able to return some of their nurturing hospitality with foods they missed, and I also loved teaching Robyn how to make them.

Chapter 7

ISTANBUL

—— ✦✦✦✦ ——

Nilgun had arranged for a car and a guide to pick me up at the airport in Istanbul. As I exit customs, I spot a woman with wild, curly gray hair who immediately recognizes me: "Zia!" she yells over the crowd. Her name is Lemika and her electric energy almost bowls me over. She speaks perfect English (and very fast), and immediately takes charge of everything. I instantly understand why Nilgun has chosen her, and by the time we reach the hotel, I've been briefed on schedules, tours, guides, options and descriptions, where it's unsafe to eat and drink, and various hotel protocols. I feel like a visiting dignitary, as my time in Istanbul has been organized to accommodate all the things I want to see and do— along with one extraordinary addition.

Lemika has personally researched the tomb of Nakshidil, the Ottoman Sultana about whom I have written two historical novels, *The Veil and the Crown* series: *The Stolen Girl* and *The French Sultana*. This was a labor of love written over a ten-year period, a story I had known about for forty years and dreamed of telling. It tells the true story of two cousins born on the island of Martinique in the mid seventeen hundreds. At fourteen years old, they secretly consult an old African Obeah woman (fortune teller) who tells them they will both be queens; one known the world over and the other more powerful but "hidden" ...no one will ever know her name. The books tell the story of how this prediction comes to pass and it is more unbelievable and fascinating than any tale I could ever invent. One of the cousins lives out her life in France and the other is abducted by Algerian pirates at the age of nineteen and given to the Sultan of Turkey as a gift where she becomes Nakshidil, one of the most influential women in the Ottoman Empire; "wife" to one sultan, secret mistress of the next and mother of the one that follows him! I wrote the books without ever setting foot in Istanbul and dreamed of one day visiting the palace within whose walls she lived for thirty-five years.

Coincidentally, Nakshidil's shrine is in the process of being restored, and Lemika's daughter-in-law knows one of the women working on the project. Lemika has arranged for me to visit the following Saturday, five days hence. She says I won't be allowed to enter the actual tomb, but I can view it from the outside and, best of all, the architect will show me photos of the interior. I am ecstatic! Lemika adds that she has gone to see it herself and that it's one of the most beautiful tombs in Istanbul; bigger and more elaborate than most others, including that of the man considered to be the city's founding father.

We arrive at the elegant Sultanhan Hotel, situated on a quiet side street and shaded by beautiful old trees one block off the busy main thoroughfare—and walking distance from The Topkapi Palace. The palace tour was scheduled for the entire next day with a guide specializing in Palace history. Today, I could either go on a boat ride up the Bosporus or a shopping excursion to the old Bazaar; I choose the bazaar.

It's a fifteen-minute walk, and on the way Lemika fills me in on the history of the famous underground shopping mall that's been in operation for over one thousand years. We make our way through main streets and then onto winding, narrow cobbled ones lined with stalls and shops. Walking is difficult through the crowds of pedestrians, and the cobbles are uneven and often slippery with spilled food and debris. The streets become even narrower and steeply sloped as I suddenly see the arched entrance to the bazaar below. A few steps later, my sandal catches on an uneven edge and I become airborne, arms outstretched and parallel to the ground. I fly down the alley and land flat out and sprawled across a table of silk scarves with a searing pain in my left arm. I'm stunned and disoriented and it's difficult to move from this awkward position. A couple of people attempt to right me when I scream, "stop!" The terrible pain in my left arm seems to be holding me down, and when I turn my head to look, I see the metal arm of a clothes rack protruding from my upper arm. I have been impaled. Instinctively, I try to remove it with my right hand, but am unable; it's embedded in my arm. "In the bone?" I think. I pull harder, causing more pain and spurting blood until eventually, I'm able to extricate it, then pass out.

When I regain consciousness, I'm seated on a crate with my head between my legs, feeling nauseous and surrounded by a crowd of people all speaking excitedly in Turkish. Lemika is by my side, holding onto me and crying. "I'm okay," I say to comfort her, but it's a lie. I'm holding my hand tightly over the wound and hear Lemika say, "Let me see it, Zia," so I slowly release my grip. Blood gushes from my naked arm and I notice blood on my foot, which also hurts, but not as much. Everyone around us begins shouting and I try to pull myself together, but it is useless. Lemika speaks with several of the bystanders, telling me that one of the shop owners has gone to fetch his car to take us to the hospital. I have no idea how a car is going to negotiate this tiny, crowded street. Still in shock, all I can do is sit there, feeling dizzy and nodding my head.

Time passes then, magically, the sea of people parts and a car appears. I am helped into the back seat and faint again as I have no recollection of the drive out of that maze. The next thing I remember is being on a main street, stopped in commuter traffic, and Lemika saying we were taking an ambulance the rest of the way. Sometime later, I remember being strapped onto a gurney and loaded onto an ambulance with Lemika sitting on a bench next to me. She is so distraught that I'm more worried about her than myself.

The ambulance delivers us to my hotel, where a doctor is waiting to examine the wound. He takes one look and says we need to continue on to the hospital. They put me back in the ambulance to negotiate traffic to the hospital where I'm wheeled into a room with several nurses. Two of them examine the wound, asking Lemika questions; then one leaves and quickly returns with an injection, for tetanus. A minute later, a young doctor arrives and examines the wound. He says he doesn't believe the metal has punctured the bone, but if so, it's only superficial. Lemika translates for him, telling me it will need several stitches and that he'll numb it, so it doesn't hurt. "Good," I say, smiling.

He smiles back and asks Lemika my age. When she answers, he stops what he's doing and asks her to repeat what she had said. Then, he looks at me with raised brows and says, "Incredible," in English. He then announces my age to everyone else in the room, and a half dozen people materialize from the hallway to see me. We all laugh, and the doctor goes back to stitching me. He asks what the secret to my youth is and I ask how much time he has. "Mostly, I just try to avoid injuries like this," I add. He does such an impeccable job that a year later there's no scar, which is extraordinary considering the depth and width of the wound.

The doctor explains that I will need to return to the hospital or visit a private doctor in six days to have the stitches removed. I also must not get the wound wet, and I'm terribly disappointed I will not be able to visit a Turkish bath. Once I'm bandaged and good to go, Lemika asks if the ambulance might be able to take us back to the hotel, since it would take two hours in traffic by taxi. "Of course," the doctor replies and I wonder how much this is going to cost.

Before leaving, we stop at the reception desk where I'm presented with a CD of my X-rays, a full report of the treatment I'd received, a seven-day round of antibiotic pills, a package of dressings and medications for my wound, instructions for Lemika (now my private nurse) on how to properly change the bandages for me daily, and a copy of the bill for my records. The total cost, including two ambulance rides, is three hundred twenty US dollars, and the woman apologizes for what she considers to be a great expense!

By the time we get back it is after nine pm, and the hotel graciously brings a tray of fruits and cheeses to my room. Lemika and I cancel the tour plans for the following day to do something easy, depending on how I feel when I get up. She offers to arrive in the morning to help me bathe and wash my hair (currently matted with blood) and change the dressing on my wound, which needs to be done every day. I gladly accept.

My second day in Istanbul is kind of a blur as I'm obliged to take a pain pill and don't have much energy. By the following day, I feel more myself and really want to get to the palace. I'm not certain I can accurately convey my feelings upon entering the massive park that is the first entrance to the grounds of the Topkapi Palace. Working on my novels, I spent hundreds of hours in libraries researching etchings from the eighteenth century to learn what the palace looked like at that time. Now, two hundred fifty years later, I am following in my character's footsteps.

I walk through the first gate and a chill runs through me as my eyes fill with tears. I stand still, and tears roll down my cheeks. Aimée, the nineteen-year old stolen girl who would become Nakshidil, stood here and saw this for the first time just as I am. The immensity of this place is initially overwhelming, and the cool green beauty of the gardens is captivating. I can easily imagine the Sultan's gazelles quietly grazing beneath these very trees. Following a ten-minute walk across the park, we proceed through the gate in the second wall, the sheer size of which is hard to imagine; eighteen footsteps from one side to the other.

Once inside the palace, the most surprising aspect is the intricately tiled walls everywhere. In fact, there are no untiled surfaces. My guide is a lovely young woman named Sanem, who explains that when I visit the bazaar, I will meet the artisan who hand-painted the tiles for the restoration. Imagine massive, thirty-foot high walls covered in tiles that look like paintings of the most intricate designs, some depicting scenes, some mythical, some sensual and all exquisite.

* * *

We spend the entire day in the palace where Aimée/Nakshidil had lived out her entire adult life. I imagine the scenes unfolding and by the time we leave, am utterly drained and exhausted. I am speechless as we traverse the park. In an effort to lighten my mood, Sanem asks if I might be interested in meeting her artist friend whose atelier is located on the outer grounds. Coskun is a well-known artist who practices the ancient technique of water painting; not water color. Florentine artisans adapted it a few centuries ago and made it famous in bookbinding.

A few minutes later we enter his small studio where an eight-year-old American girl is trying the technique for the first time. It's easy to see how gifted she is from the painting before her, and her parents stand proudly by. It's a fascinating process, using a tub of oil into which a paper is placed. Pigments are carefully dripped into the oil and manipulated with a stylus to create either a free form pattern or a realistic design. As the artist demonstrates, he creates a perfect, single red tulip and explains that tulips are considered good luck, a fact I'd uncovered years before while researching. I wander around the studio, leafing through all the available paintings and marveling at their technique and beauty. I want to purchase one to take home, but with another year of intensive travel in front of me, know this is impractical.

As we're leaving, Coskun presents me with a small piece of calligraphy he has created while I browsed. It's my name in Turkish, beautifully executed in eighteen karat gold on black card stock. I thank him profusely and we leave. Sanem asks if I'd like to stop by to meet another of her friends on the way back to my hotel. "He is the chef owner of the best restaurant to replicate Ottoman palace cuisine," she explained. "Are you serious?" I ask.

"Yes, quite," she says. "And he even speaks some English."

* * *

Fifteen minutes later, we walk into Restaurant Deraliye, a short walk from my hotel. It's an elegant, modern space with a glass wall of doors opening onto an outside dining area set back from the little side street. Necati, a handsome young Turk in suit and tie, hugs Sanem and greets me warmly, inviting us in and asking if we were hungry. "Not now, but definitely for dinner tonight," I reply.

"Well, then," Necati says, "take a look at the menu and see what looks good."

The menu is amazing, and I want it all, so he agrees to arrange a tasting of several different dishes. Unfortunately, he will not be at the restaurant this evening, but assures me his manager will take good care of me. We chat about my books and many of the palace food items I had included, which segued into a conversation about publishing in Turkey. He gives me the name of a friend of his who worked for a big publishing house and, like everyone else I've met there, suggests I publish Nakshidil's story in Turkish. She was one of the most important women in the Ottoman era, but the Turkish people know little about her. The mothers of sultans came from every country of the world, from diverse religions. But the average Turk knows only about the bloodline of the sultans, who were all either sons or nephews of other sultans. That night I walk from my hotel to Restaurant Deraliye where I'm met by the charming Maitre'D who places me at a

lovely table next to the open doors. One minute later, a
champagne glass filled with dark burgundy liquid is placed
before me. "Pomegranate serbet," my host explains. I had
made this one of Aimée's favorites in my story, and picked up
the glass, imagining Aimee, a French girl of eighteen, tasting
something so exotic for the first time. To say it was delicious
would be a grave understatement. I sip it slowly to relish every
sensation and open my eyes as a small dish of something
unrecognizable is placed on the table. When I inquire what it
is, I'm told its mashed olives with garlic, onion, goat cheese,
parsley and four different peppers. It arrives with a basket of
house-made, soft white crusty bread and a glass of Doluca
Antik, a Turkish wine from Izmir on the west coast. The
complexity of the dish surprises me despite the simple
ingredients. It does not taste like anything I've ever tasted
before, and I've eaten olives in myriad ways.

When the dish of olive delight is gone, the appetizers
begin to arrive. These include Ottoman ravioli filled with
spinach, cheese and pine nuts, baba ghanoush of smoked
eggplant with onion, garlic, mint and yogurt, stuffed into half
a ripe tomato, and my personal favorite, a tart of seven Turkish
cheeses with peas baked in filo, topped with raisins and honey.
I ask the name of this miraculous treat and am told Gem-i-in
bor-ed, which I notate phonetically. (I should note that these
dishes are brought to the table and served while The
Bachianus Braziliarus, one of my favorite musical
compositions for guitar, plays in the background. I am in
dining heaven.)

I realize that my sensory relationship with food may seem
more reliable than my sensory relationship with men, but this
thought will need to marinate a while.

* * *

I eat slowly, not finishing any of the dishes, in hopes of
being able to try everything that is still to come. The first
entrée arrives looking like a painting: half of a giant red apple

stuffed with minced lamb and beef, with currants and pine nuts. The fragrance is intoxicating, and the taste is my favorite combination of spicy and sweet. "We usually bake this in half a melon," my host explains, "but Necati did not think you'd be able to eat that much." I am barely able to eat the small portion when the next one arrives: roasted lamb shank with white eggplant purée in a puff pastry shell. The meat is so tender I don't need to chew it, and the eggplant puree is delicate and divine. I've eaten almost the entire dish when the lamb with figs, grapes, apples and honey arrives. I decide this is desert and have only taken a few bites before my host smiles, informing me there's "just one more."

I'm determined to at least taste the final dish but find it hard to tear myself away from the sweet lamb and fruit. Luckily, the entree of beef marinated in cinnamon and cumin is my least favorite, or else my stomach might have exploded. I lean back from the table and cradle my full belly, content.

I decline desert saying that the honeyed lamb had been enough.

"I recommend one last serbet," my host says, "To aid the digestion with a small after dinner wine." How could I refuse?

The dinner service lasts for two and a half hours, and when I ask for the check, I'm told there would be none; I am Necati's guest that night. I protest to no avail, and immediately decide to return the following evening so I can buy a dinner and return the favor. As I rise from the table to leave, my host places a cardboard tube into my hands saying, "I hope you will enjoy this small gift, a remembrance of your time here."

"May I open it?" I ask.

"Of course," he says.

It's a water color painting of a single red tulip by Coskun, the artist I'd met that afternoon. My jaw drops, and I gaze at it in amazement. "How did you know?" I ask.

"He is a dear friend," he replies.

I'm stunned. Istanbul is certainly a magical place.

CHAPTER 8
NAKSHIDIL

———— ✦✦✦✦✦ ————

Istanbul is a clash of cultures and I find myself both enchanted and appalled. The current president caters to the fundamentalist Muslims, while the major portion of the population prefers to participate in the modern world. The crowded streets are filled with women in European-style clothing and an equal number of women draped head to toe in black hijabs, like ghosts moving silently among the living. The style of hijab – a niqab – is so severe as to leave only a thin slit for the eyes, and most women wear glasses, either dark or clear, over the slits. The temperature hovers consistently around ninety-five degrees with what feels like an equal amount of humidity. I wear a light cotton dress and am soaking wet within minutes. I cannot imagine how hot and sweaty these women must be inside their punishing tents of heavy fabric. Lemika tells me there are three serious medical issues that result from wearing burkas: diseases of the eyes, bones and scalp. The lack of exposure to sunlight causes bones to become brittle and ill-formed while the scalp and hair suffer a variety of maladies from lack of oxygen and ultraviolet light. The distorted line of sight creates ocular imbalance and problems, which explains the ever-present eyeglasses.

Men stare openly at me with an expression of disapproval and occasionally, anger. We pass a frightening scene as an old woman with a deformed leg and wooden crutches sits on the sidewalk begging. A group of four screaming young men angrily rush to drag her to her feet. "They don't tolerate begging," Lemika says without explaining why. It is embarrassment or intolerance?

* * *

As we walk, hawkers in front of shops and restaurants call out greetings in English, French, Italian and German, hoping to entice passersby…feigning intimacy. "Hello, remember me? I remember you." I instantly learn to ignore them as if I don't understand because engaging means either being physically pulled inside or being verbally chastised.

* * *

On the other hand, the artisans I meet are gracious and genuinely interested in my impressions of their country. There are fruit juice stands on every block and the smell of freshly squeezed oranges makes my mouth water. Lemika forbids me to drink any of it, however, explaining that the glasses aren't washed, and neither are the fruits or machinery, or the hands that prepare them. "It's very dangerous to drink anything on the street."

We are on the way to visit Nakshidil's tomb and now are only one block away. "It is next to The Blue Mosque," Lemika says, "A position of great, great honor and it is bigger and much more beautiful than the tomb of our founder." We arrive at a fenced construction site with a locked gate and no one seems to be around. Walking the perimeter, we see a small guard shack from which a man emerges. He and Lemika speak and she becomes very upset.

"What's wrong?" I ask.

"The man who is going to show us the photos is not here. The guard says he has left the city for the day."

My heart sinks.

"Can we go look anyway?" I ask.

"He says no. The office is locked." She begins to argue with the guard and after about ten minutes, tells me that he said he would call someone. "I will call someone too," she tells him and dials her daughter-in-law who works with the architect. She hangs up and says with satisfaction, "Someone is coming to let us in." I love this woman and am so grateful she is with me on this journey.

We wait twenty minutes, standing in the shade and two men finally appear. Lemika cannot hide her excitement. "They will take us to the tomb and let us inside!" she whispers excitedly. "You may not take photos inside, but we can go in. This is a much better plan!"

On the short walk to the site I ask lots of questions and learn that the reconstruction began about six months earlier as part of a project to honor Nakshidil's life and that a book on her life, complete with photos of the tomb, is in the works. The men don't know who is writing it or who funded the project but suggest it may be the government. Lemika rolls her eyes at me on this and says most likely it's privately funded.

But it is clear that Nakshidil's son, Sultan Mahmud IV, oversaw the design and ordered the construction of her tomb.

Five minutes later, we stand outside another locked fence over which I can see the scaffolding that surrounds a big marble mosque. The entire building is made of white marble that is in the process of being cleaned. The classic gold scimitar and moon sit atop the round roof but there's an uncharacteristic, subtle flourish carved into the marble above the oval second-story windows.

We pass through an imposing gate adorned with gold Arabic inscriptions and enter the private courtyard surrounding the tomb. As we stand facing the actual entry to the mosque-like building, I see the same flourishes above the arched doorway, but these are painted pale blue and I immediately identify the style as Louis XVI, after the last King who sat on the throne before the French revolution, when the Sultana, then a young woman named Aimée, was stolen by Algerian corsairs.

I step inside. Overcome with emotions, I begin to weep. Her wooden casket adorned with inlaid mother of pearl, sits in the middle of the space. I turn slowly in a circle looking up at the round, smooth walls decorated in Louis XVI as well. I lay one palm on her casket and cannot stop more tears. Here is the woman whose story I carried with me for more than forty years. I hope her soul is at peace.

When we leave, I notice a building, a small replica of the tomb, on my right and ask its purpose. One of the men explains that it's the building where the caretaker lived, and I'm amazed: In perpetuity, Aimee's son has provided a full-time caretaker for her remains. How devoted must he have been and how much must he have loved her?

CHAPTER 9

KUSADASI

M y week in Istanbul was more amazing than I ever imagined and the next morning I left to fly to Izmir on Turkey's west coast, where I would meet Nilgun—the woman who made it all possible—for the first time. She arranged for a car and driver to transport me two hours south to the seaside resort of Kusadasi where I will stay for the next ten days.

Along the way, some of the scenery resembles Spain while some reminds me of California. As we near our destination, the road becomes a coast road along high cliffs, and I can see the resort town below. It is picturesque in a different way than the coasts of Italy or France, and more like Greece. The water is turquoise, inviting.

We drive all the way down to the marina and then take a steep gated road up a hill overlooking the marina. A discrete sign reads, "Kismet Hotel Guests Only" with an arrow pointing towards a gracious white plantation-style building at the top. It is almost New England in its style with green trim around the windows and doors and situated with a three hundred sixty-degree view. A circular drive leads to the main entrance with a bougainvillea-covered portico and large, glass French doors leading to the lovely lobby. The interior is

painted in soft shades of blue and white and it feels gracious
and elegant without pretension. The back wall of the lobby
and seating areas is glass, giving an unobstructed view of the
sea below. I know I will be happy here. The desk clerk greets
me and says Nilgun will arrive momentarily. I fill in the hotel
form, hand over my passport and am handed a large, old-
fashioned brass key with a big brass tag attached. I love the
retro feel of it all as the clerk says he will have the bellman
show me to my room and call me when Nilgun arrives.

The bellman opens the door to a huge suite facing the sea.
As he opens the glass sliding doors to a big private balcony
with couches, chairs and a small table, I can hear gentle
lapping waves below. Everything is upholstered and
decorated in shades of blues and white like the lobby with a
silk duvet, comfortable couches and overstuffed easy chairs.
The bathroom is elegant black and white marble with high-
end Italian amenities. This is clearly a five-star hotel and I
have been given one of the most expensive suites with an
ocean view.

Within minutes the house phone rings and the clerk says
Nilgun is in the lobby. She is an elegant woman about my age,
with long hair pulled back into a low ponytail. She greets me
warmly and we sit down on a blue silk sofa to chat. The entire
wall behind the sofa is covered with photographs and Nilgun
says, "family photos."

"Are these your cousins?" I ask.

"Yes," she says, "This was my uncle's (the sultan)
summer house. They turned it into a hotel about fifty or sixty
years ago."

There are photos of her aunts, uncles and cousins with
Prince Rainier and Princess Grace, The Queen of England,
and assorted royalty from around the world. There are formal
portraits of her aunt and uncle, the grandchildren of the last
sultan, and their families. I am bursting with questions but try
to contain myself. Nilgun and I discuss the tour plan for
Ephesus and she tells me she has found a *goulette* I might be

able to sail on for a week. I can hardly contain my excitement: my journey has become more incredible than I ever imagined. Nilgun invites me to join her and an American friend that night in her favorite seaside restaurant and asks if a short twenty-minute car ride would be all right.

When we arrive at our destination, I realize that when Nilgun said, "seaside" she meant exactly that. The restaurant itself sits on the beach, but the tables are arranged at the shoreline, on rocks over the lapping waves. I had been warned to wear beach sandals and now understood why. The three of us eat delicious seafood and drink good wine literally on the water, with the sea licking our toes under a star-filled sky.

The next day, my guide picks me up to drive to Ephesus for a five-hour tour. It would take a whole book to cover the ancient wonder that is Ephesus so let me just say that spending the day walking among the beautifully reconstructed ruins of a magnificent city that pre-dates the birth of Christ by one thousand years was extraordinary. Highlights: the ruins of the Temple of Artemis (one of the seven wonders of the ancient world destroyed by Goths five hundred years before Christ), equal-armed crosses one thousand years before Christianity emerged, images of the goddess Nike with her swan, the row of fourteen marble toilets in the boys' school bathroom, still intact, colored mosaics on the floors of buildings, roads and walkways made of solid white marble, and the amphitheater. I was left questioning how a civilization can lose the values and abilities it took to create such a place at that time in human history and why it failed to flourish. Will generations a thousand years hence look back at us with the same bafflement? I already look at our modern world that way and think we haven't learned much. How did the matriarchal society that created Ephesus in which females were revered, morph into a society that enslaves, hides and shuns them? The five women I have come to know here are all highly educated, intelligent, and accomplished, but still almost as voiceless within Turkish society as Nakshidil. I understand how their family ties keep them here and wonder what I might do in their place.

I return to the hotel in time to meet Nilgun for a drink before dinner. She left word at the desk for me to join her outside at a table on the shaded lawn. A handsome silver-haired man with a long mustache stands as I approach the table and extends his hand. "I am so pleased to meet you," he says. Nilgun says, "This is my cousin, Halim Ozbak."

I am shaking the hand of the great grandson of the last Turkish sultan.

"Please," he says, indicating an empty chair, as a waitress instantly appears, "What would you like to drink?" He is elegant, beautifully dressed in whites, and speaks perfect English with a slight British intonation. By the time my gin and tonic arrives, his sister, Hanzade has joined us. She looks like Meryl Streep's beautiful twin with silky long blonde hair and blue eyes. She is welcoming, charming and gracious and asks a lot of questions about my novels and how I did my research. She tells me that she is the narrator for a popular Turkish television series and proposes I consider the possibility of turning my story into a series for TV. I have always liked this idea and hope to one day see it as an HBO series. The thought of seeing it produced in Turkey, where it actually takes place, is incredibly exciting to me and Hanzade offers to "investigate the possibility."

For the next week, I swim in the Aegean Sea, take copious notes and naps, and sip nightly cocktails with the last sultan's grandchildren. Halim is a "car guy" and one day invites me to accompany him to visit a new private car museum that houses the collection of a wealthy friend. Nilgun drives us and we spend hours (as the only visitors) among more than three hundred of the finest specimens of cars from the beginning of car history.

One evening I venture alone to the seafood restaurant located below the hotel, on the edge of the cliff. The waiter is very flirtatious when he brings me the menu. He is proud of his English and, after perusing the menu, I ask him what is served with the fish. He replies, "First you eat the fish and then you eat me." I tell him never to say that to anyone again. He spends the remainder of the evening trying to make up for his rudeness and it is difficult to be too angry with a non-English speaker who may not have fully understood what he said. On the other hand, when I am ready to leave he once again invites me to spend the rest of the evening with him, so he probably understood perfectly. Once again, I was "fair game" as an unaccompanied tourist. Had I been in the company of a man or Nilgun, it would not have happened. It made me wonder if he would have preyed upon a single Turkish woman.

* * *

The following day, Nilgun and I finalize plans for my week on the *goulette* that will depart from the marina at Bodrum, an hour south. Since my reservation had been made so late through an unfamiliar company, she offered to drive me there to meet the people and check out the ship. "I hope it is good," she added. For what it was going to cost, I hoped so too. How much should one pay to sail to eight different Greek and Turkish islands in one week on the equivalent of a large, private sailing yacht, with only fourteen other guests? And when might I ever have the chance to do something like this again? The ship's cook would provide all meals and cocktails and wine could be purchased on board. Friends of mine in California had taken this type of sailing trip about a decade earlier and described it as the most beautiful and relaxing vacation they had ever had. The photos they showed me made my mouth water and I vowed to one day do the same. I had never done anything like it and yearned to know what it was like to live on a sailboat on a warm gentle sea.

CHAPTER 10
THE GOULETTE

S unday morning, I say goodbye to my exquisite suite at the
Kismet Hotel and head down to the lobby to see Halim
Ozbak one last time. I tell him my friend Ray in California has
found him an original radio for the classic Triumph Spitfire
he's lovingly restored, and he is very happy. I ask the desk
clerk to take a photo of us on the blue silk couch. Hanzade is
not in the hotel this morning so instead of taking a photo with
her, I shoot some of the framed photos of her and her family
hanging on the lobby walls.

Nilgun's friend Sherry enters the lobby and tells me that
Efe, my driver, broke his leg the previous night playing
basketball so she and Nilgun will drive me to Bodrum. It is a
two-hour drive that reminds me of Northern California and we
stop for a tasty lunch along the way.

When we arrive, the port town of Bodrum is bustling with
tourists. I realize this is where my favorite glass teapots and
tea glasses are made, and wish I was not traveling so lightly
and could buy some.

The u-shaped marina is filled with over forty *goulettes*
bobbing on the quay that fronts the town with an equal amount
of day tour boats and some gorgeous private yachts.

Whitewashed buildings, square and painted with narrow blue trim, step up the hillside from the wide avenue. It's a well-planned community Nilgun tells me intentionally designed, unlike the haphazard disarray of Kusadasi. We find our way to the yachting office where I sign the necessary papers and we follow an agent to the *goulette*, Hermes. It is docked alongside a dozen others with polished mahogany hulls and shiny brass and steel fittings. They are old world elegant with wide, flat hulls and not an inch of fiberglass. Nilgun and Sherry board with me to see me off and we learn that dinner will be served on board followed by an orientation. There are fifteen passengers, including me, in the only single cabin. The boat will spend the night in port and make sail after breakfast the following morning. I thank Nilgun profusely, which will never be enough for everything she made possible for me, hug them both and say goodbye. I am embarking on the next (unknown) part of my big adventure and already feel wonderful on the boat.

It is only 3 o'clock so I unpack in my tiny wooden cabin. A double mattress occupies most of the space, a funky wooden cupboard beside the bed has one shelf and rusted metal hooks on the walls provide the only places for clothes. The Spartan bathroom has a shower just large enough to stand in, a minute sink and toilet. When I bend over the sink to wash my face my butt extends into the cabin behind me. None of this dampens my enthusiasm for the trip. As a former hippie, I can do funky.

I decide to take an exploratory stroll around the marina and find a modern looking liquor store with a large selection of good tequilas directly across from the gangplank: Patron, Don Julio, El Jimador, all for 150 Turkish lire ($50.00). An ancient castle sits at the end of the marina and restaurants and cafes line the busy street. Tourists from all over the world stroll, shop and eat. It reminds me of a smaller, chicer Alghero. I make my way back to the boat, settle in to one of the wide banquettes that line the stern and order a gin and tonic from one of the three crewmembers.

Sitting on my perch at the back of the boat, sipping my G&T, and watching people stroll along the waterfront, I see a shirtless young man with the body of a Greek god. He is flanked by four young women, talking animatedly and laughing. No sooner does the thought, "why can't someone like that be on my boat?" enter my mind than he saunters up the gangplank, followed by his harem. He flips his sunglasses up onto his head, revealing eyes that crinkle just like Paul Newman's when he smiles. "G'day" he says in a thick New Zealand accent, "I'm Todd."

"And you speak English," I say, then add, "Well sort of English." He is stunning and probably not yet 30...maybe not even twenty-five. He stretches out next to me, his tanned muscled torso against the white leather banquette and begins an affable conversation, introducing each of the young women. They are all flat mates, living and working in London and he isn't paired up with any of them. Gay? I wonder.

I text Lilli and tell her that Todd rhymes with "bod" and "Oh my God" and that I want to lick him all over. Bear in mind, I would never ever actually do this with a boy/child, but I am fascinated by the fact that the feelings are never the less aroused in me. Will my hormones never calm down? I thought they surely would by my age, but they have not. Neither has my attraction to physical beauty. I have always been a sucker for a pretty face, but it also has to be smart, creative, engaging, self-aware and a myriad of other things or else it's just a toy. Playthings have a place of their own, nothing to do with relationship. I tell myself it's OK to have the feelings as long as I keep it under wraps and have no designs or expectations. I can't help noticing beauty in a perfect male specimen, can I? That doesn't mean I want to keep it. Had he been age appropriate with silver hair, it would have been a different story

As the passengers board, I meet Yves and Michela from Bologna. They are traveling with Yves' business partner, Devi and his wife, Tuna, who are Turkish. Both men speak English,

Italian, and French and of course, Devi speaks Turkish. Tuna seems quite shy and speaks no English and Michela speaks a little, but I am happy to speak Italian with her. I feel an immediate affinity for Yves, Devi and Michela who laugh easily and often, and we become good friends during the trip.

The captain tells us that Turkish law forbids passengers from bringing alcohol on board and we must order drinks through him. When I ask about the tequila, he says he'll buy it in the next port, then adds that it's very expensive. Each drink will cost me 30 Turkish lire, or $10, while other drinks are around $3. I tell him to forget it and plan to stick to G&T's instead.

At dinner, which is served on the beautiful long wooden table on the back deck of the boat, I sit next to an adorable Australian lesbian couple who later wander off with me to a rooftop bar where we pay New York prices for vodka sodas. Afterwards, we wander through the still crowded streets and I duck into a small jewelry store to buy a silver ankle bracelet. As we get closer to our boat, the disco music from across the street becomes unbearably loud. Two clubs on the same block are competing for loudness; each blasting different music. How the hell are we going to sleep? Back in my cabin, vibrating from the level of sound, I miraculously reach my daughter on FaceTime and she can hear the music through the phone! She prescribes Ambien and earplugs. The latter does almost nothing against the blaring sound and thumping beat and I pray for the pill to work quickly.

Thank you, Ambien. I fall asleep quickly and am rudely awakened by knocking on my door, which I ignore. I go back to sleep until they knock again and yell, "Breakfast!"

"I don't eat breakfast," I think to myself, too asleep to speak but now unable to fall back asleep.

Pulling on my shorts and tee shirt, I shuffle to the deck where everyone has already finished eating and order coffee. "Nescafe?" the crewman asks. "No! Definitely not Nescafe...coffee with milk." He looks at me incredulously and scowls. Apparently, this is an unreasonable breakfast request that calls for animated discussions between the server, the cook and the captain. Finally, the young crewman asks, "Turkish coffee?"

Hallelujah! Not a cappuccino but coffee nonetheless. Tonight, before I retire, I will leave instructions to let me sleep in.

After hours of preparation for embarkation, moving the boat from one side of the marina to another and going through passport inspection, we spy a small duty-free shop next to customs. A bottle of Patron coffee tequila comes back to the boat with me and the day is already looking up. I will have my nightcap tonight whether or not the captain has secured a bottle.

We sail for an hour then anchor in a small bay in the shelter of an island, diving and swimming. The water is delightful; crystal clear and a perfect temperature. Afterwards, a simple lunch of chicken cutlets, farfalle pasta and salad is served on board. We dine in our swimsuits and I sit next to Michela and speak as much Italian as I can, appalled at how much I've already forgotten.

The wind picks up after lunch as we sail towards Kos and it's a very rocky but enjoyable sail. When we pull into the harbor, the masts of another *goulette* poke out of the water alongside the dock where the boat has sunk. It must have happened recently, possibly that day and everyone speculates as to how and why. The captain announces that we should return to the boat by eight thirty for dinner, after which, we will sail to another harbor that is less rough and more protected.

I disembark with the Italians and we head down the dock. The narrow beach is covered with small tents and the closer we get, the easier it is to see its Syrian families with children and lots of young men. The old city walls are similarly populated, and as we walk toward the center of town, we pass hundreds of families camping along the path; some sleeping on sheets of cardboard. Hand-washed underwear, t-shirts, socks and shorts are set out to dry over bushes lining the path and the whole area smells of urine. These poor refugees have nothing and nowhere to go. I'm not sure how they eat, and I know they bathe at the public water fountains around the town because we've seen them. "What are they going to do with them?" I ask Yves who lives in Bologna. "What are *we* going to do with them, you mean," he replies. "No one knows."

* * *

The next morning, I am awakened by a breeze on my face and sunlight pouring through the porthole above my bed. Hearing a splash in the water I look out to see the beautiful Todd swimming by. What a lovely way to wake up.

I order a Turkish coffee and watch the server pour my morning coffee into a tiny thimble of an espresso cup. "Can you please pour into a bigger cup?" I ask. "No," he replies, "later." I have no idea what he means.

Last night I calculated that the $1300 I paid for this one-week cruise is only about two hundred dollars less than the price I paid for one week on a Seabourn cruise. The difference is this one lacks everything that cruise offered; everything. The food is mostly good, which is about the only positive thing I can say about it. It may be the worst value in the Aegean. The cabins are tiny without drawers, shelves, or storage of any kind in either the sleeping space or the bathroom. The coffee is instant, and it would be nice to have a bowl of fresh fruit during the day. Any special request is openly frowned upon or flat-out refused. One of the Italians brought his own espresso pot but is not allowed to use it. On the third day of sailing, the bathroom receptacle for used toilet paper is finally emptied. The split bamboo shades that should give shade on the back deck provide very little if any; they don't roll down easily and can't be secured while they are down, causing them to flap into the passengers. When we asked if we might have some music, we got annoying rap in

Turkish. All the passengers are growling about the lack of simple service.

The next day we reach Kos, where the same bottle of tequila is selling for 72 Euro.

We drop anchor in a beautiful little bay off Krytos, referred to as the "little Ephesus." Visible ruins of a small amphitheater and many other structures line the shore. The captain says we will return for a tour and exploration on the last day of our trip, but for now, we'll swim in the bay. Everyone takes turns diving or jumping off the boat into the clear blue water. "Now this is the way to wake up," I think. A little later, we sail for an hour to another larger bay on the backside of Symi where two enormous yachts sit at anchor. We swim, eat lunch and then swim some more. I'm getting very relaxed, which always feels a lot like lazy to me.

The following morning, the engine directly beneath my cabin wakes me when it turns on at dawn. Unable to go back to sleep, I open the porthole above my bed and the diesel fumes pour in. Pulling the pillow over my head, I hold my breath until we're out of the harbor and underway to breath freely. Watching the deep blue water pass from my porthole, I decide to brave the deck in the morning light and am only the second person up as we cruise away from Symi in a sparkling sea.

The islands here look like huge rocks jutting out of the sea. Trees appear only sparsely and where there are trees, there are towns. A little while later, we motor in between an opening that leads to a natural bay, well-hidden and chosen for protection from pirates. The sloping hillsides are tree-covered and dotted with gorgeous two-story Greek houses painted white, yellow or pale blue. Even the smallest ones have the classic Greek columns and pointed roof that mimic the Parthenon; it's surreal.

CHAPTER 11

SETTLING IN AT SEA

———— ◆◆◆◆ ————

A lovely meditation in the bow of the boat brings a hint of melancholy followed by deep gratitude: I am in heaven. How fortunate am I? When I venture forward, the breakfast table is set and the young crewman smiles and says good morning. I spy actual coffee cups (not tiny Turkish ones) at the place settings and ask if I might have a cup, to which he replies very proudly, "Of course. Which plate?" I am mystified until I realize he is asking me where I'm going to sit. I point to a place setting and he smiles broadly, picking up the matching cup and saucer. I sit at the table, not wanting to confuse him by moving around, and a few minutes later, he reappears with a full cup of brown liquid that may actually be decent coffee. I ask for honey and milk and when I've added them, and it looks just right, I sit down to have a sip. It is instant coffee, Nescafe, but this time I don't mind. I sip it slowly pretending to enjoy it and tell myself that I will have an Italian cappuccino...soon. Good coffee has come to symbolize home for me and I think it's interesting that I've come to think of Cagliari in that way. I've also begun to think of this cruise as camping out or roughing it, which makes it easier to enjoy.

They ring the bell for breakfast and people begin to arrive and sit at the long table. As Michaela settles next to me, I ask her to please only speak Italian with me today. When her husband Yves arrives, she passes it on to him, and I'm very pleased to be able to practice.

After several hours of swimming and sun in a small Bay off Symi, we set sail for Rhodes. As we motor in to the harbor we see one of those gigantic, twelve-story cruise ships already docked. I think I'd rather remember that I accidentally had sex with Keith Richards than sail anywhere on one of those. A Medieval wall protects the old town from invasion and stretches as far as I can see, but it is useless against this modern behemoth. Despite the allure of a donkey ride, I decline joining the girls on trip to a point of interest and wander into town on my own, in search of a real cappuccino. Fortunately, it's easy to find a cafe that serves Illy coffee made in an actual espresso machine. Taking a sip, the thick rich foam tastes like heaven in a cup and makes me moan like I'm having an orgasm. A perfect cappuccino feels almost as good as being in love and I wonder if caffeine and milky foam produce endorphins.

* * *

My next objective is to find a new bikini and a cotton dress made in Greece. The bikini remains elusive, but I find the perfect flowing summer dress made on Corfu, under which I need not wear a bra...heaven again. The shop owner, a lovely young woman named Katerina, asks how I stay in such good shape and I recommend yoga. In return, she tells me to read the psalms of David for a calming effect. I have little knowledge of the Bible and make a note to consult one. What I know of King David is from the Richard Gere film and based on that, it's hard to imagine his psalms as anything but arousing.

As I begin to wander back towards the marina, I see an interesting shop that does not resemble any of the commercial ones I've passed for the last two hours; it's actually a gallery of paintings and jewelry with the most interesting and beautiful array of things I've seen anywhere in Greece. The female artist, who makes big repurposed necklaces from bits of old ones, sits in the back, waiting to see if I'm seriously interested in any of her pieces. A small glass display case holds one-of-a-kind silver pieces including a silver Coptic cross. The shop owner (and artist of the paintings that hang on the walls) explains that the pieces in that case come from the estate of the most famous jeweler on Rhodes, who died several years ago. The original boxes bear the store's Art Deco logo inside on white satin. Since I just photographed the exact cross at Ephesus for my daughter, Ariane, I buy the pin for her on the condition I can have it in one of the original boxes. It makes me happy to find a perfect present for her and I take photos of the pieces I find interesting instead of buying them for myself.

I spent an interesting evening the previous night alone on the boat with Yves and Michela from Genoa. She is a multi-generational Genovese and he is a French Jew born in Egypt, who moved to France when he was four. When his father died a few years later, his mother remarried an Italian, and moved the family to Genoa. He was educated in private schools in Switzerland, where he met the fascinating Turkish (also Jewish) Devi. They are old school chums going back more than thirty years, who are now in the chocolate business together. I like them all very much and feel so happy to be speaking Italian!

One of the things I love most about travel abroad is the wide diversity of people. When people immigrate to the US they drop their cultural identities to become "American." Turkey, Greece and Italy are a mix of all the cultures that invaded them for centuries, making them much more complex than the American melting pot.

When we sail from Rhodes to the Turkish port of Dacha, it resembles a small town in the south of France and I'm thrilled there are no tourist shops on the wharf, no goods made in China, no peddlers trying to sell you things you'd never buy, and no hawkers outside restaurants shouting out at passersby in a variety of languages. The thing I love about travel is getting a true sense of a place and the history that makes it what it is, how things become as they are and how that in turn makes the inhabitants the way they are. This is why I prefer to travel off the beaten path; it's the only way to really see a place. I try to imagine myself living there or being from there and wonder how the place might have fashioned me to make me different than I am. It helps me understand the differences and similarities in human beings and ultimately, within myself.

* * *

Last night, Yves told me the yachting company that owns this boat had recently purchased it for one hundred thousand euro. My business-woman's brain adds up the cost per cabin multiplied by twenty cabins, which makes that amount seem paltry, and I begin to fantasize, design and decorate the one I will buy and moor somewhere in Italy. Surely, I could interest some boat lover to invest in that, I think.

"Who will run it?" Yves asks me.

"I'll hire a captain," I reply.

"Or marry one," he says jokingly.

How great would that be? This may become my new dream plan (I mean the boat.) I would turn the quarters in the bow into my private living space and be the on-board chef cooking delicious meals from fresh ingredients bought along the way and fish caught in the sea. I'd invite local archeologists and anthropologists along to entertain the guests with historical items of interest. I can picture myself being very happy and possibly even alone and happy this way. I must be making more progress.

* * *

We arrive at a gorgeous small inlet with clear turquoise water. When I dive in, I'm stunned by the color and the white sand bottom that must be fifty feet below. There are only two other day boats in the inlet that leave as we arrive. Hussein, from our crew, dives into the water, and swims a big rope to the rocky shore, where he loops it over a jutting rock. It must be too deep to anchor and we are mooring here for the night. It's nice to think that we'll be somewhere quiet with no other boats or shore noises. This is how I imagined the entire trip and I am happy to have at least one night like this.

Dinner is one of the best so far; grilled sea bream with a spicy sauce of peppers and tomatoes, fava (not the bean but the lentil), sea beans (Turkish seaweed that I love) with tomatoes and garlic, and the ubiquitous salad that I don't bother with. I sit next to Yves and Michela and get to know them even better, learning that she works as an assistant to a climatologist who does government-funded research on climate change. They tell me about the "Pastafarian religion" started by an Italian comic who actually received legal certification. He fought (and won) to be allowed to wear the Pastafarian symbol, a *scola pasta* (pasta strainer) on his head for the photo on his driver's license. The followers worship and pray to a plate of meatballs and spaghetti in the sky and Yves and Michela become my new best friends. We exchange numbers and email addresses to stay in touch. Tomorrow we return to Krytos, the mini Ephesus.

I've been meditating most mornings on the bow of the boat and doing yoga and a little Pilates every day and am feeling great. I'm a darker tan than I've been since I lived in Malibu forty years ago, and my hair is bleached out to platinum from the sun and salt water. Yesterday, I almost bought a gold belly chain like the one I wore in 1971, the era I'd most like to revisit. That was the beginning of my "free spirit" lifestyle as a newly liberated (divorced) young woman raising a daughter by myself. As a professional dancer/singer, I was in perfect health and condition, working in musicals, taking dance classes and working out at the Beverly Hills Health Club, writing songs and recording demos, traveling with one of my older millionaire lovers between Hollywood, Lake Tahoe, Hawaii, Santa Barbara and London, learning and riding Hunt Seat Equitation with my daughter who had just started competing, doing Erhardt Seminars Trainings that opened my mind in a brand new way, socializing with polo players, movie stars and Hollywood hopefuls (many of whom would become famous). I had a wide variety of lovers of different ages, types and interests, the eldest being the "primary" with whom I am still very close. I had just read Anais Nin's diaries and had begun keeping a journal, into which I entered a lot more questions than answers and my life was fueled by hope and aspirations. Looking back on that time, I miss the plethora of possibilities and the drive I had to taste the world. Forty-five years later, despite my many achievements, life feels smaller.

If I could look any way I've ever looked in my life, I would pick that period of time. I wonder if I'm unconsciously trying to recreate it with my dark tan and long sun-streaked hair. The last three lovers I've had were 41, 39 and 38 so maybe I am regressing. Tonight, I realized I have not cried for missing Luke in almost a week and it feels like I'm making progress but not sure why. I also wish I knew what happened to that belly chain.

We spend the night moored in a cove that is blissfully quiet; the only sound water gently lapping the rocky shore, to which we were tethered (and the ropes making the mouse noises). No earplugs are needed, and I sleep through breakfast, have a "rubbish" cup of coffee as Yves would say, and dive into the clear water for a morning swim. Tonight is our last night at sea and I'm definitely ready to go "home" to Cagliari – but I'm not going yet...first, Istanbul, where I hope to have meetings to explore book and television possibilities for my historical novels.

* * *

An interesting night: We are tucked into a lovely little bay and after taking a final swim with Michela, I go below to shower and change for dinner. I hear the dinner bell and move above to the table, which has been laid out when we hear the engines start. "What's going on?" I ask. "We've run out of water," the captain says. As soon as we depart the protected bay, the seas become very rough...all the furniture on the deck slides from one side of the boat to the other. A few passengers panic and I hold onto the side rail like a carnival ride, grinning from ear to ear.

An hour later, when we still haven't found land, the sun sets and it gets very, very dark. Suddenly, in the distance, lights begin to appear on what looks like a wide white beach. It is a deserted port with a new sea wall and empty bay. We motor in just as complete darkness swallows us up and the howling wind picks up even more. Even in the protected bay, the wind and sea bounce us around all night. It's too bumpy and noisy to sleep so Devi and I drink most of the coffee tequila until after two a.m. and I gratefully sleep until eleven.

* * *

In the craziness of the storm, I forget that my iPad was plugged in to the only outlet in the salon. When I wake up and enter the salon to retrieve it, my heart sinks. Everything is wet, and my keyboard has drowned. I try it, type a vowel that reproduces thirty clones. It is useless. Maybe it's a sign; a reflection of my life being dead in the water. If I wanted a blank slate, I now had one. This is an opportunity albeit a forced one, a chance to erase everything I've thought until this point; rethink my relationship to sex and love and prioritize what I want going forward. Could I learn to do this? Do I have a choice?

CHAPTER 12

ISTANBUL AND ATHENS REVISITED

— ◆◆◆◆◆ —

Nilgun books me into a hotel for two nights, conveniently located near the publishing house that might want to publish my book in Turkish and Lemika has promised to help me find a new keyboard for my iPad.

The mall we visit is enormous, with expensive designer shops like Channel, Gucci, and Cartier. I've not been surrounded by luxury like this in a long time and at the moment, can't imagine desiring these things. The Apple store is a three-story glass structure with long lines of people everywhere. I've brought my dead keyboard with me and ask a floor person if I have to stand in line to get a new one, to which she happily responds, "Oh, no. They are right here on the wall. And I can take your credit card right here."

"Wow! That was easy," I say, and in another minute, we are out of there.

After Lemika leaves, I set up my iPad and begin to write. It doesn't take long for me to discover that the keyboard is in Turkish. So, it's back to the store to ask if it can be adapted to English. Unfortunately, it can't so I'm still without a keyboard but hopeful that the tiny Apple store in Cagliari will have one.

The next day, before my meeting, Lemika and I have a lovely lunch at a Thai restaurant, a real treat for me. Afterwards, we wander past high-end shops in an upscale neighborhood I'd not previously visited. Passing a small jewelry store, a ring catches my eye. "Oh, it's beautiful, let's go see it," Lemika suggests. We enter the shop and before I know what's happening, I'm holding it in my hand. "I am not buying a diamond ring," I say to Lemika.

"Of course," she replies, "but it is very unusual."

I put it on my finger and am transfixed looking at it. It's like a meditation mandala, with three circles of tiny blonde diamonds and an outside ring of white ones. "It's much too expensive," I say to the sales woman, handing it back. She looks at the tag, which I'd not even seen and says, "The price is twenty-two hundred euro."

"Good," I say, "Way too expensive."

"I can do better," the saleswoman immediately says.

"I'm afraid it would have to be a lot better," I say with a laugh.

"I can do fifteen hundred," she says.

"No, still too much, but thank you for trying," I say, turning to leave. It's not a bargaining tactic; I seriously have no intention of buying a diamond ring.

"How about eleven hundred?" she inquires.

It stops me in my tracks. I take the ring back and put it on my finger. "Was it made here?"

"No," she replies. "It was hand made by an artisan in Florence, Italy."

"Of course, it's Italian," I laugh. "Like most of the things I love."

I'm transfixed by the concentric circles of diamonds set in an uneven circle of pink eighteen-karat gold and I can't help but fall in love. I look at Lemika and say, "I might be crazy, but I think I could use something to love unconditionally right now and I can't travel with a dog." I turn to the sales woman and say, "I'll take it."

And that's how I acquire a blonde diamond and eighteen karat gold ring that centers me and has a calming effect, just like a mandala. I wear it on my wedding band finger, and it comes to symbolize my marriage to Italy. I think it also represent my full commitment to myself—a precursor to finding the right man. And my belief that I will one day find the perfect union.

* * *

The meeting Hanzade had arranged for me with the publisher does not bear fruit, as they do not publish historical fiction. But my Turkish friends assure me that it would never publish as it stands because it is too controversial for the fundamentalist government. After the disappointing meeting, I treat myself to the full Turkish bath treatment at The Sultanamet, one of the oldest bathhouses in Istanbul that Nilgun says is also the most luxurious.

The moment I enter the quiet, elegant space, I relax. It's a large open square built of pale sandalwood latticed walls, with luxurious white cushioned banquettes. I check in at reception and choose the "ultimate classic bath with massage" from the menu of services. An attendant escorts me to a wooden changing area, where I leave my clothes in a wooden locker, slip into white slippers and wrap myself in a big soft white cotton blanket. Reclining on a banquette, sipping mint tea, I wait until another attendant collects me, gently taking my arm to guide me into the *tepedarium*, a warm room to acclimate to increased temperature before being bathed. I recline on another banquette with more tea, almond stuffed dates and tiny candies. Now I feel like the main character in my books. Ten minutes later, my attendant escorts me into a white marble room with marble benches along three walls that are interspersed by ornate brass faucets and sink bowls. She unwraps me, hanging my blanket on a hook and bending to remove my slippers, then leads me, naked, to a marble bench (shaped to hold the curve of buttocks) where I sit. She turns on the faucet and fills a large copper bowl with warm water, which she then pours over me. Once wet, she lathers my body with a large soft sponge and gently washes me, using the bowl to rinse me. She shampoos my hair supporting me with one arm while she gently rinses away the suds. It's an odd sensation to be bathed like a child, and once I'm able to relax, brings back feelings from early childhood. I can't describe the basic feeling of being loved and nurtured and am so moved I cry.

The final part of the treatment is what separates the Turkish bath from all others. You lie on a heated white marble slab as an attendant waves something that resembles a large white linen pillow case back and forth over your body. A blanket of warm foamy bubbles floats onto your skin covering it in a warm, silky cloud. I have never experienced the depth of relaxation that follows.

* * *

I have no memory of the short walk back to my hotel where I fall into a sound sleep. Luckily, I had texted Nikos the night before to arrange for him to meet my flight in Athens the next morning where, once again, I would spend the night to catch an early flight back to Cagliari.

My flight arrives in Athens about eleven thirty a.m. and when I pass through customs, it's easy to spot Nikos, looking gorgeous as ever with an ebullient grin. He takes my bags and squeezes my arm as we walk out of the airport. When we get to his car, he asks where I want to go. "How much time do you have?" I ask. "All the day," he replies. "Wow," I say. "Can you be my tour guide?"

"Yes, where you want go?" he asks.

I'm starving and tell him the first thing I want is lunch. "What you like to eat?" he asks. "Souvlaki!" I say. He laughs, "Ok, I take you to best souvlaki in all Athens, OK?" I feel like Shirley Valentine again.

As we begin to drive, he watches me more than the road and says, "You so beautiful. I like these color green eyes and gold hair. Very beautiful woman you are. I am happy you are here." So am I. "California woman all like you?" he asks. I laugh and tell him, no, I'm the absolutely only one and we both laugh.

We drive for about thirty minutes past the urban sprawl that is Athens, and the density of houses covering the hills reminds me of Los Angeles. I learn he'd been a pro footballer who retired from the sport to buy his taxi business and start a family. His children are the loves of his life, and he speaks openly about how devoted he is to them. The sexual tension is palpable through all the talk of family and jobs, with Nikos testing the water to be sure he's reading my signals correctly and not overstepping the boundaries between chauffeur and passenger. Once he is certain I'm on board, he turns on the charm full blast.

* * *

He winds his way expertly through the insanely crowded streets of downtown Athens, miraculously finding a parking space a short walk from the restaurant. As we navigate the crowds of tourists and sellers, I observe multiple spinning racks (like the one that stabbed me in Istanbul), displaying hundreds of hand-painted wooden dildos. Dildos being sold openly on the street! They are neatly arranged by size from the smallest (pinky finger-sized) on the top to the largest (forearm-sized) on the bottom. Painted garishly with designs of flags, scenery, psychedelic swirls and frolicking classical Greek gods, they remain the single memento I regret not having bought. I look at Nikos and ask, "Dildos?"

He laughs and says, "Of course. You in Greece now!" He wraps an arm around my waist to pull me against him as we walk, and I wonder what the single word to describe Athens might be. Aphrodisiacal?

Minutes later, we're seated at an outside table on a bustling street filled with restaurants. Nikos orders for us and a short while later two huge plates of souvlaki arrive. It looks like enough for four people, and I dig in, eating as much as I can. We discuss the sites I hope to see and how best to accomplish this, settling on the Acropolis as the first since it will take at least two hours.

Finishing lunch, we get back into the car. He sits in the driver's seat and turns towards me, smiling as he reaches across the seat to slide his big, tan hand up my naked thigh under my skirt and asks, "Where you want to go now, Acropolis or hotel?"

Duh. "Hotel, please," I reply.

"Good," he grins, then kisses me deeply on the lips.

"Condoms?" I ask. He puts one finger up and says "wait," then jumps out of the car and runs to a newsstand, returning with a box of condoms. It makes me wonder how often he does this, but I don't really care.

I gave him the hotel's address at lunch, and he questioned the location. Now, as we drive into the neighborhood I understand why: every visible surface is covered in graffiti; every inch of every building. I have never seen graffiti like that, block after block. "Is this neighborhood okay?" I ask. "Not at night," he replies. "You not walk out at night here. Bad boys here at night. If you want go out, take taxi from hotel and back." Right, I think.

No surprise to find that the hotel is also sketchy, and had I not prepaid a non-refundable amount on line, I would tell him to keep driving. That's the last time I'll trust hotels.com reviews. How lame or drugged was the guest who said, "excellent location to walk everywhere?" Luckily, I have other more important things taking my attention.

We take the miniscule elevator up to the third floor and open the door to my closet with a bed. At least it's clean and air-conditioned. Nikos hugs me and we fall, laughing onto the single bed. I excuse myself to use the bathroom, and when I open the door, I have a view of the bed directly in front of me. Nikos is lying on his back naked, propped on pillows with one arm crooked behind his head; his hairless, darkly tanned athlete's body stretched out with a giant erection pointing to the ceiling. His penis is unusually long and curved up at the tip. "That's going to feel interesting," I think.

"Will you do something for me?" I ask. He pauses and nods his head.

"Please only speak Greek now," I tell him. He laughs and says something I do not understand.

"Good," I say, and we begin to kiss.

I haven't been kissed well in a long time, not felt a man's hands on my body and he feels delicious. He is very athletic, and apparently likes the fact that I'm petite and lithe. He picks me up easily, so I can wrap my legs around his waist as he enters me, carrying me this way around the room (what little room there is). We laugh like teenagers and it's over too quickly. I'd prefer to have enjoyed him slowly. On the other hand, I *do* want to see the Acropolis and Parthenon.

At the end of the day, overwhelmed by ancient Greek culture, Nikos drops me at my hotel, so he can return to his kids. He reminds me to only leave the hotel by taxi. We kiss goodbye and I thank him for making my day in Athens better than the usual tourist agenda. He promises to pick me up in the morning and take me to the airport.

I follow his advice and take a taxi to Syntagma Square to find dinner and safely stroll around. After a wonderful dinner in a "farm to table" restaurant, I wander through the shops, not terribly interested in any of the things they sell. Earlier, I had passed the impressive Hotel Bretagne and want to see the inside. The lobby tastefully screams *five-star* and the marble bar looks elegant and inviting so, I take a seat and survey the beautifully displayed bottles of high-end alcohols. Spying a bottle of Don Julio, I order one neat. The liveried bartender bows slightly and addresses me as "Madame," which I am. Had he seen me impaled by Nikos a few hours earlier spinning around the tiny cheap hotel room, he might retract it. I smile to myself. He pours a generous amount of liquid gold into a crystal snifter and sets it in front of me on an embossed coaster, along with a silver dish of cashews and another of perfect green olives. I know I'm going to love this place. Why am I not staying here? I ask myself, already knowing the answer. It makes me question my life choices, and I know exactly how my life would be had I chosen differently, stayed on other paths. I would be a guest at this hotel as I had been many times in the past. But would I be as happy as I am now? Wait...am I *really* happy? Sometimes.

This thought brings me to a philosophical quandary and the very reason I rarely ask myself "what if?" There is no positive aspect in regret. At that very moment an age–appropriate man enters the bar; a six- foot tall, extremely handsome, silver-haired, beautifully dressed gentleman with his look-alike adult son. They sit in big easy chairs next to the bar and begin a conversation...American, upper crust, possibly Connecticut. I expect a tall blonde Grace Kelly look-alike to enter and join them, but none does. This is the type of man my friends think I belong with and I sometimes fantasize about: a successful, well groomed, American grown-up who stays in luxurious hotels ...like I used to. The universe is sending me a message and I don't know what to do about it. Obviously, it's time for me to figure this one out. I'm afraid if I dwell on it now, I'll begin to cry so, I polish off my tequila, pay my tab and exit through the exquisite lobby to get a taxi back to my hovel.

The next morning, I replay that scene and instead of asking myself what if, ask myself why not? This seems like a good place to initiate a change of heart, an attitude adjustment that might allow me to materialize a satisfying relationship in the future. It occurs to me I may have been protecting my broken heart since the breakup with Luke and meaningless sex with younger men was safe compared to falling in love again.

I feel excited to return to Italy and I am downstairs when Nikos comes to pick me up. We drive to the airport with our hands resting on each other's thighs and share one good kiss before I leave the car. "You see me on Facebook, okay?" he asks. "Okay," I say. "Remember wife see it too," he reminds me. I laugh and tell him not to worry but warn him to behave himself and not to be a bad boy too much. He puts his hand over his heart and nods slowly, with a sheepish smile. Another hug and I'm inside the airport, on my way home to Cagliari. *Grazie Dio!*

CHAPTER 13
RETURNING TO CAGLIARI

I time my return to Cagliari to arrive on the same day that my friend Carole arrives from the UK. She is the friend I met the previous spring at One World language school, who'd taken me to visit Pula for the first time. Now she is planning to spend two weeks there and invited me to join her. We will take private Italian lessons, a great way to rekindle my Italian language skills.

September is still summer and after our morning language class we usually go to the beach. It's an easy pace and we quickly adapt to the rhythm of relaxed days ending with gin and tonics, and home cooked dinners followed by a stroll or bike ride into the village to use an Internet cafe. We love our trips to the handsome butcher's shop and occasionally take a day trip to another beach or place of interest. Still without a keyboard, I continue my holiday from serious writing and focus on Italian instead. I surf apartment rental sites and go into Cagliari a couple of times to see apartments that are not to my liking. Toward the end of my two-week stay, I find what looks like an interesting apartment for a very good price and Carole and I decide to check it out.

Following a fifteen-minute climb up to the top of the tallest hill in Cagliari called "The Castello," we stop in front of an impressive new wooden door and ring the bell. The housekeeper opens the door and before even stepping foot inside, I love it. Situated one street below the castle where the reigning monarchs had previously lived, the three-story building is seven hundred years old and newly restored by a Milanese architect. The inside is modern, with clever touches of the original three-foot thick stonewalls peeking through, high beamed ceilings, an all-glass bathroom, two big French windows with traditional heavy wooden shutters, two flat screen TVs, a stereo, and brand-new appliances that include a state-of-the-art chrome and red espresso machine. There is a large painting of a gold Buddha on one wall of the bedroom, which pleases me immensely since I've always kept a gold Buddha in my home. The bedroom is decorated in the same colors as mine in California; white walls, charcoal accent-wall and bed covers, and red sheets. I want this apartment. We ask the cleaning woman, Marisa, if anyone else is interested and she says another woman has made arrangements to spend the night and then will decide if she will take it. I tell Marisa that I don't need to test it out and ask if she can put in a good word for me, adding that should I be the new tenant, I will keep her on as housekeeper. She will see what she can do. I am certain this is my future home and have the feeling I've lived in this area before, in another life perhaps. Something about it makes me feel perfectly at home…as if I belong here.

* * *

I spend the next week communicating with the landlord, and finally get a commitment to move in three weeks hence. I book an Airbnb in the marina district until I can move, which turns out to be incredibly noisy. The Marina is a busy touristy area that winds up the hill above Via Roma, the avenue along the port. It's the only area "downtown" with ethnic diversity, which I enjoy: East Indians own small souvenir shops and markets, and Senegalese street sellers congregate. There are also bars where local young hipsters hang out. Even going to sleep at one or two a.m. as I normally do, I have to close all the windows and shutters and use ear plugs. I don't know how anyone lives here in the summer, when everything must stay open for ventilation. I also don't understand why the city of Cagliari does not have a noise code like most residential areas in other cities. After the bars close it becomes cacophonous, and I'm relieved to be here only for three weeks.

Continuing daily classes at One World I meet several new students, a few of whom will become close friends. Irina is a stunningly beautiful half-Romanian, half-Russian woman in her late thirties who lives in Luxembourg. She is as intelligent as she is beautiful; fluent in seven languages and an interpreter for the EU. She'll be spending six weeks in Cagliari to get certified at the highest level of fluency in Italian, and she'll become my personal interpreter and Italian coach—as well as my closest friend. Felicia, from Mexico, is also in her mid-thirties, and her level of Italian matches mine, which puts us in the same class. The three of us quickly become inseparable. For a few weeks Franzi, a schoolteacher fluent in four languages and on sabbatical from Germany, joins us. Being around these accomplished, bright women is inspirational and gives me hope but also makes me feel like I've begun my language study fifty years too late.

Felicia lives on Poetto Beach and introduces us to a crew of locals from that area, opening a whole new world for us outside the city. We meet a group of wonderful women who range in age from mid-thirties to late-fifties, all of whom love to party. Sometimes they even bring their husbands along, and we begin going to local events, concerts and clubs that we'd otherwise never know about. I name these local girls "the Italian gang."

Irina also knows a lot of Sardinians from her previous visits to Cagliari and introduces us to a whole new circle of artists, photographers, painters, filmmakers, and musicians, many of whom live in my favorite neighborhood, Villanova. My horizons expand exponentially, and life becomes more interesting and a great deal more fun. Our new friends introduce us to traditional Sardinian style restaurants where they simply ask if you want meat or fish when you enter. You are seated and choose red or white wine, which arrives in a carafe along with dishes of olives and potato chips. Very soon platters of food begin to arrive and continue for the next three to four hours. The dishes are delicious, and the cost is about twenty euro per person, including many carafes of wine.

It is at the first of these feasts, with ten other people, that I meet the talented musician Rinaldo Pina, who will become my closest non-English-speaking friend. He reminds me of my father (who I adored) in size, looks, and demeanor, even his laugh. This explains why I fall in love with him, albeit platonically. He is fifty-five years old, the same age as Luke, and before becoming a musician, had been the captain of a sailboat! He would be the perfect boat captain for my *goulette,* and we could play and sing for the guests after dinner. Rinaldo still owns two hard-to-come-by slips in Cagliari and we discuss the possibility.

* * *

The month of October remains unusually warm, and knowing winter will come soon, everyone spends as much time as possible at Poetto beach. At night the little kiosks along the beach turn into clubs with music, dancing and mojitos. It's here that Rinaldo names Irina, Felicia and me the "Almodovar Girls," and we try very hard to live up to the name. I move into my new apartment and invite everyone over for margaritas and guacamole. My new friends bring so much to my life; the female intimacy of close girlfriends, sharing confidences and discussing our feelings and the challenges we face, laughing at ourselves and with each other. Our close friends are mirrors for us and as a single woman, alone in a foreign land, this is one of the things I missed most. Through them I am buoyed up about my singing, my writing, my former accomplishments and the wisdom I am able to bring to the table. They are the sounding boards for my confusion and doubts about men, sex and relationships...even if they don't hold the answers. The next six weeks are the happiest weeks I spend in Cagliari, and I have no idea how we manage to squeeze so much life into every day.

We spend three hours in school from ten to one thirty then go out for lunch. After lunch, we head to the beach or sometimes have lunch at the beach. If we plan to stay at the beach all evening, we start cocktails around six or seven. Sometimes we return home to nap before going out for the evening and reconvene around nine, depending on the night's program. Whatever we choose always includes three things: food, drinks, music and often dancing. Irina and I usually end the evenings by two or three while Felicia (bless her Latin heart) continues until dawn. Consequently, she is always late for school, arriving hungover with wet hair, heavy eyes and a triple espresso. No one feels the least bit sorry for her.

I've also begun tango lessons again with Tonio and am making good progress. We dance for an hour twice a week in the early evening before I meet up with the girls. Yet our relationship is now completely different. I find myself annoyed by him when we aren't dancing, by his narcissism and need for drama. Tango requires the woman to surrender and trust her partner completely; something I normally find difficult to do with men. When I allow my annoyance to enter the dance, I'm unable to follow. Surrender was the very thing that attracted me to tango in the first place. I'd subconsciously sought out a practice to help me to learn to trust a man. This is a revelation, as it addresses what psychologists might call my core issue – the most important lesson I've come here to learn.

Since Cagliari is a small city on a small island, it happens that Rinaldo's group of friends include many of Irina's from Villanova. In fact, we discover that Rinaldo produced the

Beatles reenactment concert in Piazza San Domenico that my friend Annie had brought us to! He has recently been named artistic musical director for a new small community theatre and asks me to join him for opening night. When I arrive, he and two other musicians are on stage playing so I wait until they finish, then walk up to say hello. Rinaldo, who speaks no English, is very upset with me and—after asking him to speak more slowly—I understand that he meant for me to sing. We laugh and apologize to each other profusely, and he asks the others if they can stay longer to accompany me. They unpack their instruments (sax and bass) and Rinaldo makes an announcement to the audience, then hands me a microphone. He and I had fooled around with the Eva Cassidy version of *Over the Rainbow,* so we begin with that, followed by Queen Latifah's version of *California Dreamin'* both of which I've only sung once before with Rinaldo. Now there are two other musicians playing along for the first time and trying to follow. Without a proper rehearsal, none of us did our best, but hey, I got to sing to a large audience of Italians and christen a new theatre in Cagliari!

* * *

I'm now living in the Castello area of the city where the palace of the queen, Regina Margherita, was built more than seven hundred years ago. In the last century, it was converted into Il Palazzo di Governor, a municipal building that currently offers cultural events. The building sits atop a wall over two hundred feet above street level, in a piazza with a church and another building that's now a museum. The piazza is about one large city block long and equally as wide, with two sets of steep steps leading down to Via Nicolò Canelles, the narrow, cobbled street directly below where I live. In the opposite direction from my house, the street winds down three blocks to the top of Mussolini's Bastione where, theoretically, one can stand on the large white marble piazza for a three-hundred-degree view of the city below, including the salt flats and the sea. The salt flats are home to a huge flock of flamingos numbering in the thousands. Unfortunately, the Bastione has been under construction and closed for over two years. After a whole year of walking past the site every day, I can understand why it is taking so long – actual work rarely happens.

I walk down my street every day to and from school, stepping into doorways and pressing my back against the stone to allow cars to pass. It's a miracle that cars drive here at all through the warren of tiny one-way streets barely wide enough for a normal sized vehicle. Most people have smart cars, mini Fiats, scooters or motorcycles. One brave soul flew past me on a bicycle the other day and a large, black BMW sedan, driven by a man I hoped might become my future husband, stopped to give me a lift.

Each day as I make the trek down, I ask myself why I don't hitch a ride with one of the passing cars or motorbikes. People are very friendly and neighborly here and it would be easy, if I knew how to ask. Last week, when I was running late, the big BMW passed me and pulled over in front of the Bastione entrance. Two men exited the car, and the driver was very attractive – think Richard Gere in a beautiful Italian business suit. They immediately got back into the car as I rushed down the steps past them and I decided that if they came around the corner, at the bottom of the steps, I would ask for a ride. Bingo! They did, and I approached them. As I got into the back seat, I thanked them profusely and explained that I was late for school. A barrage of questions followed. Where was I from, what was I studying, how long had I been here, how long was I staying and where did I live?

Later, I tell the Almodovar girls about my handsome driver and they are appalled I did not get his contact information. Seriously? What might I have said in two minutes of speaking rudimentary Italian? "Can I please have your phone number, so I can call you for a date?" For the next few weeks, I look for him and his car whenever I walk anywhere but never see him again. Irina says, it is "another greatest love story that never was." I am happy to look upon the chance meeting as an intimation of the future rather than a missed opportunity; another handsome, age-appropriate man to dream about – another possibility to light my way.

* * *

In mid-October, The Almodovar Girls come to an end when everyone leaves, and I take ten days to travel to Firenze and Bologna. I'll spare you the travel log of incredible museums, sites and shopping in Firenze but share three outstanding out-of-the-way places that are a must for any traveler. The first is Ristorante O'Munacielo, located on Via Mafia 31 near piazza Santo Spirito. They serve black crusted (not burned) pizza made by adding finely ground charcoal to the dough for the purpose of digestion. It must be true because I was able to eat almost an entire pie by myself, about three times more than usual. The pizza with burrata, sautéed fresh porcini mushrooms and black truffle sauce was simply the best pizza I have ever eaten. Second, Trattoria 4 Leone, is a two-minute walk from the Ponte Vecchio, serves the best *frito misto* (mixed fried foods) a combination of rabbit, chicken, porcini, and vegetables, I've ever eaten. The Florentine steak and whole lobster over pasta were also stellar and enough for an entire table. Third, Golden View looks like and is a touristy bar and restaurant two blocks from the Ponte Vecchio. I do not recommend the restaurant. However, the bar is outstanding for several reasons, the first of which is the very capable bartender (an oddity in Italy). The décor is upscale and modern with a wonderful sunset view, and during what we would call "happy hour" from five to eight, they serve an abundant buffet of fresh appetizers with cocktails for a total price of ten euro. My friends and I called this dinner on several occasions.

After leaving Firenze, I spend four days in Bologna with my new friends from the *goulette* trip, Michela and Yves. I explore the beautiful city with Michela as my guide and of course, eat my first authentic Bolognese sauce which I love. We also cook several meals together and I teach her how to make my pan-fried meatballs.

I am happy to return to Cagliari and start Italian and tango lessons again, but I miss the Almodovar girls and look forward to visiting Irina in Luxembourg soon.

* * *

On Thanksgiving Day, my California friends, Ray and Carla, FaceTime to wish me happy Thanksgiving. They look so cute, calling from their bed as soon as they wake up. The nine-hour time difference always makes it morning for them and early evening for me, and they knew I'd be missing friends and family. They are right – I've kept myself as busy as possible doing very un-Thanksgiving things. So, my day began with a (disappointing) manicure followed by lunch with Lili at Mamma Mia's, which is never disappointing.

As the holiday evening progresses in California, my daughter Ariane is getting ready to start cooking. She has made herself chopped liver from the turkey, which is a tradition I started eons ago, and when she calls me, I have a hard time holding back tears. My seventeen-year-old grandson, Nico spends ten minutes grooming himself before he will let me see him on his iPhone. This is the same young man who at sixteen would not leave the house to go swimming until his hairstyle had properly dried into place. During the eight months I have been gone, he has morphed into a very handsome young man. I miss them a lot but know that they are not children anymore and wonder how I will fit into their lives going forward. Grandmothers experience the empty nest syndrome too; the "Who am I if no one needs me?" blues.

CHAPTER 14

NOVEMBER GIRL'S NIGHT IN LUXEMBOURG

——— ✦✦◆✦✦ ———

I'm at the Cagliari airport waiting to board my Ryanair flight to Luxembourg to visit Irina. I'm bringing a panatone from Antico Cafe, two kinds of truffles (a pâté and a cream sauce with porcini) and a bottle of Argiolas sapa. I couldn't decide which to get so I bought them all – always the best rule to follow.

I stopped into Antico Cafe this morning after getting a blow-out at the salon next door, ate a panino with cappuccino and luckily, checked my emails to find a message from Marco saying the boarding passes he printed out for me last week were wrong and he'd scooter over to bring me the new ones. Three minutes later, as I finished paying my bill, he taps me on the shoulder wearing his big lovely grin. He is so sweet and enjoys his job so much. I am happy to be going away on one of his journeys for a week over Christmas, and today he tells me to be sure to bring a red dress for an anniversary party that will take place on the Sunday after I arrive – The Olympic Village resort in the Italian Alps is celebrating their ten-year anniversary of hosting the Olympics.

* * *

Predictably, the Ryanair flight is an hour late. When we finally board the plane, my seat is surrounded by six screaming Italian children and their equally loud, yet ineffective Italian parents. Thankfully, I have my ear buds handy. The captain, having made the "sorry we were late so please take your seats as quickly as possible" speech four times, now announces today's flight time will be *two* hours instead of the usual 90 minutes. Oh joy. The flight attendant asks the loud family to be quiet during the safety announcement, *twice*, yet the children continue to yell back and forth.

I plug in my ear buds and crank up the music of Eros Ramazzotti. Try to imagine my excitement when I realize I understand more than half the lyrics. This is a first, huge step toward comprehension of the Italian language!

As we deplane in Frankfort Hahn airport, the sky is filled with "cream of fog soup" (Tom Robbins) and the air is freezing. I get a message from Irina saying she may be a bit late because she wanted to stop at the post office to pick up my fur-lined parka that my friend had sent from California. Then I get a Vodafone messages saying that I've used up all my credit, so I'm without communication. I sit down at the end of the only corridor with a view of all entrances and ten minutes later, Irina comes running down the hall with her arms open. Moments later we are settled into her gorgeous Alfa Romeo Giulietta sedan, headed to Luxembourg to join three of her closest girlfriends at Mamacita's, a real Mexican restaurant with a good selection of tequilas.

Parking the car, we then tear open the box with my coat.

The fox-lined hood instantly repels the cold and my whole body relaxes.

Mamacita's is both modern and cozy, and two beautiful young women wait for us at a high-top table in the bar. I survey the tequilas as we enter and spot the familiar tall, blue bottle of Corallejo Reposado...yes!

The food is delicious. We eat too much, drink too much, talk non-stop and laugh a lot. The bright company of smart funny women is like a tonic for my soul and I feel instantly at home in this new country. After several hours, we kiss goodbye with future plans to see each other over the weekend.

* * *

Today Irina and I drive to the town of Trier, just across the border in Germany, for the annual Christmas market. The town is storybook charming, with a large main shopping area for pedestrians only and beautiful shops. I buy a great pair of stretchy black pants and then see a familiar looking sign; "T.K. Max," the European version of our own T.J. Max. In we go, and in a few minutes, I have found a soft warm faux fur hat and cozy suede fur-lined mittens.

It's very cold, but the sun is shining as we head into the throngs of people eating and drinking at the outdoor Christmas market. Everyone holds little red mugs in the shape of an old-fashioned boot, filled with *glühwein,* hot mulled wine that tastes as strong as it smells. Irina and I share one with our delicious fat sausages, pan fried potatoes and mushrooms with a killer-good mayonnaise cream sauce. We are both very happy...even though I'm not fond of German cuisine. They know sausages though – and Christmas.

We shop until dark, then head back to Luxembourg and meet one of Irina's friends at a favorite restaurant, Come à la Maison, a large furniture design warehouse that has morphed into a very popular night spot. Like any warehouse district, it's difficult to find without signage and only a giant table lamp on the sidewalk pointing the way. The side door leads through a long hallway, decorated with serendipitous objects d'art that instantly call Malone to mind. The three dining/sales rooms are spectacular with huge thirty-foot ceilings hung with varied chandeliers and candelabra. Big and small dining tables with non-matching chairs are scattered throughout and shelves of wines, paintings and objects d'art line the walls. Everything is for sale and I would be very happy with all of it in my home – if I had one. The host seats us at a table in the middle dining room with a partial view of the open kitchen where a half dozen Italian cooks are busily sautéing, and I am in heaven again. "I love this place," I say.

The next morning, which is Sunday, Irina asks why I must return to Cagliari so fast, imploring me to stay. In less than ten seconds, I accept. Ryanair only flies out on Monday and Friday, so we make a call and book a flight for the following Friday. I am happy to be here on so many levels. Last night I went to a Pilates class with Irina! Luxembourg is a stunningly beautiful city whose inhabitants speak three official languages: English, French, and Luxembourgish. It is also the seat of The European Union, which makes it very international and a stark contrast to Sardinia – which as we've seen is very provincial and where things rarely work. The diversity of the culture soothes my soul. I'm looking forward to my Christmas ski week in the Alps and plan to return to Luxembourg to spend New Years' with Irina.

* * *

I have spent my entire life moving from one type of environment to its opposite: from the wealthy WASP enclave of Bedford Hills, New York where I grew up, to a kibbutz in Israel; from the West Village in New York City to Malibu Beach; from the wooded hills of Mill Valley, California to the streets of downtown Chicago; from a home on a golf course in Fort Lauderdale, to the high desert of Crestone, Colorado, and then the alpine mountains of Crested Butte.

The pendulum swings from urban chic to wilderness. It's a pattern I have long been aware of. I think it's linked to my need for diversity. My "favorite" locale or style of home has changed so much throughout my life, yet I love moving from the stimulation of the city to the deep solitude of the country. Now I'm repeating this pattern on my year abroad.

In Sardinia, I fall in love with Cagliari, Pula, Villanova and the Castello. All of them have ancient picturesque cobbled streets that I love walking and visible history everywhere in the bombed out or crumbling, antiquated buildings and piazzas. I love the soft pastel colors of the ancient walls, the tiny unique neighborhood shops and churches, and the crowded, helter-skelter alleys and streets.

Luxembourg is the antithesis of all that: well-planned, spacious, elegant, gracious, chic, modern, clean, upscale and international, multi-cultured, filled with big green trees and parks, luxury automobiles all shiny and clean, and gloriously beautiful. There are restaurants from around the globe, movie theatres that show films in multiple languages and a gigantic French supermarket, Auchon, with the most incredible selection of gourmet foods I have ever seen under one roof, including an entire aisle of foie gras, my sinful favorite food. Irina takes me there when I decide to stay for the extra week and I'm able to find everything I need to make a Mexican feast for her and four of her girlfriends. I make everything from scratch, starting with the Cadillac margaritas, guacamole and chips, chicken tortilla soup with queso fresco and avocado, chicken enchiladas smothered in tomatillo salsa verde and topped with a dollop of crème fresh, rajas, pico de gallo salsa, and a crisp romaine salad with buttermilk ranch dressing. The girls are from Romania, Poland, Greece, Estonia, and Brazil, and have never tasted authentic Mexican food. Everyone raves and leaves nothing, and I have a new group of girlfriends who are smart, well-traveled, interesting, funny and beautiful.

While I love the provincial, old world quaintness of Cagliari where I am able to live inexpensively and simply, I immerse myself fully in the cosmopolitan luxury of Luxembourg. Perhaps, the way to honor my duality is to live somewhere like Cagliari and travel to exotic, luxurious, cosmopolitan places. This concept excites me until I consider my family and friends in the U.S. What will I choose in the years ahead?

* * *

Being in Europe has made me realize how much more I want to see of the world. But, by this point in my year abroad, I already know I don't want to travel alone anymore...not abroad anyway. For one thing, it is incredibly stressful to drive on highways or fast roadways in a foreign country without a co-pilot, even using a GPS. Dining alone in casual restaurants and cafes is ok but I don't enjoy dining alone in fine restaurants. Even shopping (which I happily do on my own) is more fun with someone else.

After two weeks of socializing, shopping, cooking and enjoying the diversity of restaurants in Luxembourg, I go home to Cagliari; determined to study hard and spend as much time as possible with my Italian friends before leaving for my ski holiday. With that in mind, on my last night I accept an invitation from the Italian gang to join them at B Flat for disco night with Non Soul Funky. The place is packed, and when the band finishes their last set, they invite me up to sing the blues so, I actually get to sing at the most elegant nightclub in Sardinia!

This week's exciting news is that in preparation for the wet winter, I discovered a way to take a bus from the supermarket downtown where I do major, weekly food shopping, all the way up to Castello! Without the bus, the last three trips took me forty minutes to walk home dragging fifty pounds of groceries uphill in my Gimme cart. I arrive home soaked with sweat and exhausted. Riding the bus was like a miracle and will transform my ability to shop and my dread of it! Pre-bus, I spent more time deciding if an item was worth schlepping than I did shopping.

Rinaldo comes home from a weekend in the hospital for "stomach pains," looking rested and relaxed. They told him it was "nerves" which equals "stress." It affects his stomach and digestion, so he is being careful about what he eats and promises to start yoga and meditation. While cooking lunch for us he asks in stilted English, "You are wasp?" I do not understand the question. He says very slowly, "Wide-pro-tes-tan," I double over laughing and ask where he'd heard this, and he says he read it somewhere online. It is a perfect example of the limitations that arise between people who do not speak each other's languages and reminds me how difficult it would be to enter into a romantic relationship with a non-English speaking man.

As part of his new relaxation program, we take a ride an hour outside the city to visit his brother's horse ranch in Maracalagonis (which I finally learn to pronounce after much hysterical laughter from Rinaldo). It is a beautiful country horse property that reminds me of Northern California, with a rambling ranch-style main house, two small guest cottages and several horse barns. It is the kind of property I would be happy to live on, and I try to imagine what that might be like. I picture myself there and feel it's too isolated; not a place I would enjoy living alone. I keep returning to this quandary of single versus alone with no idea how to solve it short of manufacturing a perfect mate. At least in the city, I may be isolated inside my apartment, but once I step outside and I'm around other people.

This is a strange moment in my life, a kind of holding pattern, which usually feels uncomfortable to me. However, this time, I recognize it as a precursor to change; I become a bystander, an observer in my own life, patiently awaiting the outcome. It clearly is not a time for decisions, so I simply gather possibilities and wonder how it will all turn out.

CHAPTER 15
BARBAGIA TRAVELOGUE
—— ◆◆◆◆ ——

Two extraordinary days in Barbagia, the central mountainous wine-growing region of Sardinia, an absolute must-see for anyone visiting the island. The region's name, given by conquering Romans, comes from the word *barbaria,* or barbarian; their description of the region's nomadic sheepherders. Twenty-eight picturesque small towns, each situated atop a hill, host weekly festivals of art, food and music during the fall. *Autuno in Barbargia* (Autumn in Barbargia) is the perfect time to visit.

Bill and Jess join me and twenty Italians for a day tour to visit three towns, each famous for a specific thing. Atzara is home to the art school that produced Sardinia's most famous painter: Antonio Corriga. The town itself is a work of art: colorful houses and neatly paved flat cobbled wide streets are a modern version of the original with even paving.

Next, we stop in Teti for a pre-arranged lunch in a charming restaurant on the edge of a steep cliff overlooking the surrounding hills and valleys. The altitude and cold air make it feel like Switzerland. We feast for two hours on the best food I have eaten in Sardinia: prosciutto, salame, olives, small round red peppers stuffed with salty fish pate, pickled cardoons and porcini, bread and a delicious red wine, fresh and creamy sheep burrata is unlike any I have ever tasted! In the U.S., this would be lunch – but here in Italy, it's just the warm up before the hot appetizers begin to arrive: baked focaccia stuffed with porcini and cheese, cut into small slices, and an exceptionally light lasagna of wild mushrooms. The pasta is next; *fregola,* the classic Sardinian shell-shaped pasta with red *sugo* and bite-sized pieces of *cingiale* (wild boar) that melt in my mouth.

After ninety minutes of eating, the main course arrives: platters of the most delicately cooked quail I've ever tasted, in a light brown sauce that is mopped up with pieces of bread, chunks of roasted wild boar, slices of beef sautéed with onions and porcini – and more pork with roasted potatoes, just in case anyone is still hungry.

Just when we think we can't eat another bite, little bowls of freshly cut fruit arrive with tiramisu, and grappa. "We will all sleep on the bus ride to the next town," I say to Jessica, and we do just that. Teti is famous for its food and should be a mandatory stop for lunch or dinner on any Sardinian itinerary.

By the time we arrive in Olzai, it's beginning to get dark and the temperature has dropped dramatically. Once again, the streets look newly-paved, with smooth flat cobbles, and all the buildings are pristine. An ingenious deep man-made ravine has been cut into the mountain, through the center of town, to allow the river to flow freely through it without fear of flooding. I have never seen anything like it. The walls on either side are about twenty feet deep and the top becomes a bench that lines the one-way, drivable/walkable streets on either side.

A full moon shines through the slightly misty evening sky as we walk up one side of the ravine to the craft fair where a group of musicians are playing Sardinian folk music. I am stunned by the assortment of unique hand made goods. The handbags are works of art made from cork, leather, snakeskin, natural wood, and rocks, so unusual I would buy several if there was a reasonable way to send them back to California. There's jewelry designed on ancient Etruscan pieces found on Sardinia; statues and symbols that predate Christ by several thousand years. The one I regret not buying depicts a female deity and may be the precursor of the Christian cross: a woman (with prominent breasts) standing with open arms. I had taken photos of these same statues when I first saw them in the archeological museum in Cagliari because they felt familiar and evocative to me.

My second visit to Barbagia, on January seventeenth, is to witness an ancient pagan ritual predating Christianity by more than one thousand years. In Sardinia it is called Carnivale and precedes the time of Lent; we know it today as Carnival. The primary images of "carnival" are the masks, and I'd never really understood where they came from. The Sardinian version explains that in pagan times, one day each year was put aside for people to commit any crime, or do any damage they wished, on the condition that they behave for the rest of the year. On the "get out of jail free" day everyone wore a disguise to make them completely unrecognizable.

Like all pagan rituals adapted by Christians, the masked day of chaos eventually transformed into a parade to honor Saint Anthony. However, in Barbagia, the traditional worship of Prometheus, the God of fire, is still carried out *in its original pagan form* and this is what I wanted to see. I had previously seen photos with images the likes of which I had never seen: the masks and costuming were so evocative and familiar, but I knew I 'd never seen anything like them. The strong reactions I sometimes have to ancient places and artifacts always intrigue me. Are they past life memories, examples of a universal consciousness or what?

The seventeenth of January is Saint Anthony's day in the village of Mamoiadas, and the men divide themselves into two different groups: the Mamuthones and the Issoladores. These were the photos I saw. Mamuthones dress as ominous wild animals, covered from head to toe in longhaired black sheep skins with over one hundred pounds of brass cowbells strapped to their backs. Frightening hand carved black wooden masks cover their faces, making them completely unrecognizable. Locals say this group represents the people of Sardinia who have been invaded by one civilization after another for millennia. The invaders are represented by dashing, handsomely-dressed Issoladores, who carry rope lassos blithely "herding" the wild Mamuthones as they capture and "flirt" with their womenfolk. I was roped by one and flirted with by many, much to my delight.

Dozens of bonfires burn throughout the where people gathered congenially for warmth. Locals pass among visitors, offering homemade wine, and since we've been told it's rude to refuse to drink, we're all slightly tipsy by the time we make our way to the top of the town.

All of the restaurants are closed due to the festival which makes absolutely no sense to either Christina or me, until a local woman explains that the locals gather to eat a big meal prior to the festivities. What about the thousands of tourists? The few small bars serving drinks and panini are so overcrowded it's impossible to enter – so basically, we drink homemade wine for four hours on empty stomachs.

At 2:30 we move towards the place where the costumed Mamuthones and Issoladores will emerge, in full regalia, securing a good spot on the narrow-cobbled alley, next to the huge wooden door where they'll exit. By 3:30, at least fifty more people have crammed into the narrow alley and Christina and I have a simultaneous realization: When the participants emerge, we will be ensnared in the throng following up the alleyway. "I hate crowds," Christina says to me.

"Me too," I reply. "I'm too short to fight my way through and can never see anything." No sooner are the words out of my mouth than we hear the loud clang of bells from behind the big wooden doors.

The crowd is so thick it's impossible to move as the doors open and the people crush each other against the stonewalls to allow the participants to emerge.

The scene is other-worldly and strangely silent as the last Mamuthones pass and I am lifted by the pressing crowd into the flow. My feet barely touch the ground and as the crowd turns left onto the main street and an entire block passes before I can move out of the crush onto a side street to catch my breath. I can't see my friends in the crowd that has now swelled into a thousand or more. The steeple of the church where the crowd is headed is visible, and the rhythmic clang of bells as the men jump in unison quite clear. I climb up onto an elevated cross near the church, to get a view over the heads of the crowd as my phone rings; It's Isa asking where I am. "Up on the cross," I reply, thinking, just like my last marriage.

"Stay there," she says, as if I have any intention of doing otherwise. Again, I wonder what draws us to these ancient rituals, what meaning do they have in our modern lives?

Fifteen minutes later the streets clear as the Mamuthones move toward another fire site. I backtrack to where we'd been waiting and a minute later, we're all reunited. Christina is carrying a glass of beer. "I found an empty bar," she says, with a big grin, "While everyone was watching the procession."

"Did they have any food?" I ask.

All in all, it was an experience unlike anything else, and I wish I could have seen more. However, even my brief encounter was strangely haunting, a glimpse into the ancient past of a people and place an outsider rarely gets to witness and for a brief moment, I felt I belonged. If you go, bring food.

CHAPTER 16

PRAYING TO THE VIRGIN, WISHING ON A STAR

Today is December eighth, a national holiday in Italy celebrating Mary's immaculate conception. I guess no one ever bothered to do the math, considering Jesus was born three weeks later.

As I sit in my apartment reading emails, I hear a voice over a loudspeaker reciting a blessing in Latin. Peeking out my door, I see a procession led by a priest in full regalia, being followed by about one hundred people, moving down the narrow, cobbled street. I join the parade down to a small church one street below my house and sit in the last row of seats (no pews here), as the congregation sings, prays and makes obeisance to a small statue of the Virgin Mary. Wait, isn't worshipping false idols what God warned humans *not* to do? It also brings back snippets of my youth when most of my friends were Roman Catholic. I used to spend quiet time in prayer at the local Catholic church, St. Francis of Assisi. I loved the smell of the incense, the muted light filtering through the stained-glass windows, the smooth polished wood of the pews and the soft worn velvet that padded the rail to cushion my knees when I knelt to pray, comfortably resting my elbows on the second rail. It was a space perfectly designed for contemplation; even in the dead of winter, it felt warm and inviting. Like the song says: "I stopped into a church I passed along the way, the preacher likes the cold, he knows I'll want to stay."

Now in this tiny Sardinian church, my eyes tear up and I ask myself what is it that still draws me to this? Hope. Hope for forgiveness, for redemption, for answers to questions that have none. Church is a place of wishes, just like a star-filled sky; no one truly comprehends either, but we harbor a desperate desire to understand and to heal. Praying to the Virgin Mary is no different than wishing upon a star and in one-way or another, all human beings do it. I send a wish to be filled with love.

* * *

I am really dancing tango and it feels natural, easy and very intimate, different than any form of dance I've ever done. The spontaneity and lack of choreography makes it both difficult and exciting. And I'm now able to understand the very Zen aspect of it; everything happening in the moment. If I am not present for each moment, I don't get the subtle signals the dance requires; an ability to move without thought, to simply "be one" with my partner.

I've begun contemplating options for my exit strategy after this summer and am hoping to find a writer's residency for a month or two to ascertain whether or not the copious notes I've been taking might actually become a book. I will spend the entire month of June in Tuscany with Ray and Carla from California who I haven't seen for a year! The bigger question is: where do I want to live when I return to the states? At the moment, I cannot imagine where. How will I create the reality I want if I can't imagine it, I wonder for the umpteenth time? "Visualize the end result," I hear a voice say. Okay. This is how I want to feel: happy, loved, physically strong, financially secure, wildly engaged in life, and hopeful for a bright future. I vow that this is what I will focus on from now on. Let's see what unfolds.

I write each statement of feeling on a post it and stick them up around my house then wonder if this includes a relationship.

* * *

It's 1:40 in the morning and the drums have finally stopped. Kettledrums, I believe, accompanied by a screaming voice through a microphone. I hadn't felt like going out tonight after a great tango lesson, so I made some fava bean and artichoke pasta and snuggled into the couch to watch a remake of a Noel Coward movie with Colin Firth. I love being able to dance with Tonio without socializing with him and feel happy to be alone; no longer interested in sex without love.

At midnight, I heard what sounded like gunshots, but were actually fireworks, and then church bells began to ring wildly. I wondered if it was a holiday, then vaguely recalled someone recently mentioning an old pagan day of celebration but it is too late and too cold to go outside to investigate.

* * *

Yes, last night at midnight, was the beginning of some saint's day and that's what all the noise was about. Bill and Jessica told me that they were passing through Piazza San Giacomo very late and the whole place was filled with people dressed in black with thin black masks like the ones on the Sardinian flag so there must have been an old pagan festival that (per usual) the Catholic Church attached a saint to and made it a religious holiday—just as they did all year long with Christmas, Easter and even Halloween. Everyone loves a party, and no one really cares why.

Bill and Jessica texted this morning to say they are going to a concerto near my house at eleven a.m. so, when I wake up at 10:30, I quickly dress and walk around the corner to meet them. The theatre is the same one where I saw my first concert in Cagliari with Paola six months earlier and the haunting sound of the *launeddes* had made me weep.

We leave the concert hall at 11:45 to walk down to Villanova and catch Rinaldo's Suono al Civico concert and get a cappuccino at Florio. Tonio immediately finds me and stands next to me as the first song begins. It is glorious to hear Italian opera sung by and Italian tenor in the most charming piazza in Cagliari. However, the soprano is weak and should never have attempted *Summertime*. Later that night, at Rinaldo's Sunday tea, he asks if I liked it, and I make a face, as do the other guests. I ask why as director, he allowed her to sing it. "She wanted to," he replies, adding that he really didn't have a say in her choice of songs. "Why not?" I ask. "Isn't that part of your job as director?" He replies with the Italian shoulder shrug. There are a lot of things I don't understand about Rinaldo, and probably never will, due to our inability to have deep conversations. Nevertheless, we are extremely comfortable with each other and always make each other laugh, no small feat considering the language barrier.

At the end of the concert, I introduce Tonio and Rinaldo and Tonio invites me to join him to eat ricci in the marina, giving me a chance to try the infamous sea urchins all Sardinians revere. The urchins are tiny, and one has to carefully extract the minute pieces from the delicate shell with an itty-bitty spoon. They are delicious and taste like little bites of the sea, but it would take a hundred to make a full meal. Luckily, there is pasta with sea urchin sauce that is wonderful although everyone agrees it does not contain enough *ricci* and Tonio promises to make it for me "properly" after the New Year. No dish is ever made as well as either he or his mother makes, but he has yet to cook for me.

Ricci is a seasonal treat only available from December through March in makeshift white tents along the marina just outside the city. Today is the perfect day to sit outside; sunny and almost warm with a calm sea and no wind. We sit and eat for a couple of hours, and after lunch, Tonio and I take a *passegiatta* along the marina walkway until he begins to tire and says he needs to lie down. Tonio always needs a nap after lunch, so we chose a park bench and he lies down with his head in my lap while I sit looking out at the sea. I watch all the people strolling by: couples, families with children of all ages, grandparents, and even some runners. After about ten minutes, I become extremely sad, suddenly aware that I am missing the depth of intimate human contact. In fact, I'd missed it for most of my life. It was, I knew, caused by my inability to trust, and fears left over from a difficult childhood. Tears roll down my cheeks, as I mourn all those years without a deep love, the very thing I hadn't even known existed until I met Luke, six years ago. Now I long to be held in the arms of a man who knows who I am and feels the same way. I miss being loved and loving someone that way, but now that place inside feels like a vast emptiness. Life didn't hurt as much before I knew that this kind of happiness existed. These days Luke has shut down and avoids relationships and I fear I'm headed in the same direction because the relationships I've found on this trip aren't in that same category.

* * *

Even with all this sadness, I have a very full Sunday: a piano concert in Castello, an outdoor operatic concert in Villanova, eating *ricci* in the marina, and Sunday tea at Rinaldo's with a group of his friends

The next night turns into something truly special when I pop in for a short visit with Rinaldo around 5 p.m. We chat for an hour before his friend Lello, another musician, calls to say he is coming over. Rinaldo picks up his guitar and begins playing Norah Jones, "Don't know why," asking if I know the words. I don't, but we print them out just as Lello arrives. I sing a few lines and Rinaldo adjusts the key, then I really sing it. It feels perfect, just like the first time I sang *California Dreamin'* with him and we were both surprised. Lello picks up the other guitar and I sing it again, accompanied by them both. We are all very pleased with the sound, so I print out words for two more: *Turn Me On* and *Lone Star*. The boys get a kick out of *Lone Star* because it's so country. I don't ever remember feeling so good singing songs for the first time. We are having such a good time we play until midnight after having pizzas delivered and taking a dinner break! Rinaldo and I now have seven or eight songs we love doing together, and when we face timed today, he suggested the two of us do a "Concerto in Balconi" in the spring! I am grateful to still have my love of singing—music fills me up and takes me to that place of pure bliss and contentment.

CHAPTER 17

NOT SO HO, HO, HO

W inter is transforming Cagliari into a ghost town and making the trek between school in the marina and my apartment in Castello a real chore, especially in the rain and wind. Consequently, I discontinue classes, preferring private lessons at home with a tutor, Isabella. She's both excellent and affordable, so we set up a schedule taking us to Christmas; the holiday I have seriously begun to dread.

Knowing that Christmas away from my family and alone in Italy will be challenging, I've decided to go somewhere exotic. I tell my friend Marco, a tour operator, my criteria: I want to be with single people from around the world, to eat good food, have interesting places to walk day or night (a nearby village or town), and Internet in my room so I can write and communicate. A spa would be icing on the cake. He does some research, and we meet at Moonshine, a little "American bar" near his office to discuss what he's found.

I introduce Marco to the lemon drop martini and after several, I agree to prepay for a week at an all-inclusive ski resort in the Italian Alps. The Alps sounds incredibly romantic, and Marco knows one of the hotels, which he describes as "very international and filled with people from all over the world." It's the Olympic Village where the athletes had been lodged during the 2006 Olympic games, and I begin to get excited. I've never been there and recall scenes from movies like *The Pink Panther* and old James Bond films. Even though I don't downhill ski anymore, I can cross country ski ...in the Alps, which will be amazing!

I buy thermal underwear, long wool socks, a pair of Uggs, a fake fur hat, mittens, gloves and a good sunscreen. I'll spend the week of Christmas at the resort and leave the day after for Luxembourg to spend New Year's week at Irina's. Her friend Marc is hosting an intimate New Year's party at his house with live music and exotic foods, and he's asked me to sing!

I fly to Turin and take a two-hour bus ride to the resort, excited by the chance to see the iconic mountains but we climb higher and higher without seeing snow. There's no snow anywhere, only brown winter grass and dirt. To make matters worse, all the majestic pine forests are dead or dying from invasive moths whose white tents are plainly visible atop the still living trees. The Alps are doomed and dying, and a sense of dread creeps into my bones.

Arriving in Sestriere, in the dead of winter without snow, is a sad sight; it looks nothing like it did during the 2006 Winter Olympic games that I'd avidly watched on TV. I'm overdressed and sweating in my warm winter coat and Uggs. As I enter the lobby to check in, a swarm of twenty guitar-wielding teenage boys almost knocks me over. The adjoining bar is filled with fifty animated teenage boys for a teen music school event that fortunately ends the following afternoon.

I'm extremely disappointed to discover the "quiet room" I've specifically requested is about a half mile from the lobby, and unlike the advertisement promised, it does not have Internet access. "I was specifically told there was Internet," I say. "There is," the desk clerk replies, "in the common areas," the ones filled with teenaged boys and their guitars. Well, I think, at least they're leaving tomorrow, and all will be well.

"Tomorrow," the young woman behind the desk reminds me, "we begin our weekend of anniversary celebrations so, please read the schedule of events, so you don't miss anything." OK, I think, this should be fun.

Marco had described the large buffet-style dining room as a "great place to meet other guests," because the tables are unassigned and communal. In actual fact, it feels like a school cafeteria. I remind myself that the teens will be leaving, certain that things will turn around. At this point, the cup is still half full.

I go to the bar for a quiet after dinner drink and it is filled with teens. "Is there an adult bar area?" I ask. "Of course," the bartender replies, "this is it."

The next morning, I make the trek to the dining room for a coffee (which I was supposed to be able to make in my kitchenette, but there's no coffee pot or coffee.) The only coffee in the dining room comes from a do-it-yourself machine, dispensing a brownish substance no respectable Italian would ever drink. I take one sip and dump it out, asking a waiter if there is any *real* coffee anywhere. "Of course, in the bar," he replies.

I'm paying for bad drinks at night and marginal coffee in the morning, with no Internet and no snow. But today everything will change when the new "international guests" arrive. And change it does...

The day is bright and sunny, and I need a good walk, so I climb the hill to town. On the way, I pass the main ski area that is sparsely covered with a thin strip of artificial snow amidst bare brown hills. I order a coffee at a café with a view of the slope, sipping it as I watch a few skiers wind their way down. It feels like spring in the Rockies, without snow or green trees, and I become very melancholy. This feeling is exactly what I'd come here to avoid, so I need to do something about it. Determined to make lemonade, I walk back to the hotel to scope out the new arrivals.

A throng of people fills the lobby; young Italian couples with toddlers – lots of them. Music is blaring in preparation for the night's festivities and I go back to my room to write until it's time for the cocktail party that will kick off the weekend's special anniversary events.

With much trepidation, I squeeze into my Spanx and pour myself into my red dress; a simple, long-sleeved sheath of shiny red spandex that hugs every curve of my body. Looking at myself in the mirror, I hope I don't look like an old tart and pray for the courage to appear in public. Ultimately, I take comfort in the fact that everyone will be wearing "fancy red dresses," and mine will just be one among several hundred. Also, the new guests I've seen are young, Italians who will all be wearing sexy red dresses. So, I step into my red fuck me pumps and head directly to the bar for a "shot of courage" before making my appearance.

The lobby and bar are packed with young parents and toddlers, not what I'd imagined at all. "It's only eight o'clock," I think. "They'll all be asleep after dinner." I down my shot and head for the elevators that will take me to the cocktail party. When the elevator doors open on the ground floor lounge, I instantly see I am the only woman wearing red. My first impulse is to turn around and run back to my room to change, but one of the young hotel interns has seen me and is coming my way.

"Great dress," he says.

"I was told everyone had to wear red," I say.

He looks dumfounded. "Really? I think everyone wears red on Christmas Eve."

Oops. Now I really feel out of place, certain I look like a high-end hooker in the crowd of young families. "Where are the cocktails?" I ask.

He points across the room. "I think there is prosecco over there."

I should have known there would be no actual "cocktails" as we know them. Taking a deep breath, I try to "own" the dress but feel very out of place and conspicuous. I also feel a hundred years older than everyone else, and drink two glasses of prosecco too fast. When music is blasted to announce the beginning of the performance, I perch gratefully on a ledge, out of the way where I can watch. This gives me a chance to survey the crowd, which looks entirely composed of young Italian couples with toddlers—an observation that's confirmed when we all move to the cafeteria for dinner. In true Italian fashion, two hundred screaming toddlers run amok without parental control, and the dining room devolves into utter chaos. How am I going to handle this for three meals a day for the next five days? I'm trapped in the exact scenario I had specifically wanted to avoid. How could Marco have gotten it so wrong? Did the lack of snow prompt the hotel to advertise a special family package rate? I carry my tray of overcooked chicken breast and vegetables, seriously considering skipping dinner, when I notice a narrow doorway to a small dining room. I see three tables of employees with a vacant seat at one, and the young women smiles knowingly and nods when I ask if I can join them. "It is quieter here," she says, and I roll my eyes. That little side room will become my go-to spot for all meals.

By the third day, I'm so upset about the lack of Internet I speak with the hotel manager and explain that as a writer, I need access, without dozens of screaming children running around. Thankfully, he's very understanding and offers me one of the unused conference rooms in another wing of the hotel. It's a large room with two hundred seats in neat rows, two long tables at the front of the room, a comfortable padded desk chair, and a private bathroom. The Internet is reliable and fast, and I work on my notes, answer emails, practice yoga and Pilates, and stream episodes of TV shows. For the next two days, I leave the room only to eat, sleep or take a walk into town. This is nothing like the exciting vacation in the Alps I'd envisioned, but it will have to do.

Christmas Eve arrives, and I scurry off to my private room directly after breakfast to do some Yoga and write. The morning passes uneventfully, and after lunch I walk into town, a mistake because everything is decorated in anticipation of Santa's arrival. By the time I get back to my conference room, the gloom has set in. I try Face Timing Ariane, Carla, Irina, Lili and Rinaldo but can't reach anyone. I sit at one of the tables at the front of the room of empty chairs looking up at me and it hits me hard. Once I begin to sob, I can't stop: I am alone in the Alps without snow on Christmas Eve.

I cry all afternoon until eight o'clock, when I know if I don't go to dinner, I'll be going to sleep hungry. My eyes are red and puffy and the last thing I feel like doing is interacting with other humans, but there's no choice. I trudge back to my room wearing sunglasses and give myself a little pep talk. I shower, put on some make up and give thanks for being female so I can do that. Donning a pair of beige jeans, I remember I had brought a silly Christmas t-shirt from H&M in Luxembourg. It's white cotton with short sleeves and a huge bow design of red and silver sequins across the boobs. It looks absolutely ridiculous, which cheers me up and makes me laugh at myself.

As I approach the dining room, the greeters are lined up to welcome the guests. Every woman is wearing a festive red dress. Screw it, *I* have a red sequined bow across my tits. I lift my head proudly, smile and even say "Merry Christmas," never suspecting the present that awaits me inside.

The dining room is the usual chaotic mess of screaming toddlers with the addition of red balloons, but there are no seats in my secret alcove, so I take one at a long table in the main room. An obese middle-aged mother and father sit at the opposite end of the table with their equally overweight twenty-year-old daughter. They are bent over their plates, shoveling food into their mouths without speaking, and I'm about to burst into tears and run screaming from the room when the lovely hotel manager approaches, and asks if he can join me. "Thank you," I say. "I'd be happy for the company."

"Would you mind if my friends join us?" he asks.

"Of course not," I say, noticing the two handsome men.

The dark one wearing a wedding band sits on my right, while the handsome blonde with green eyes, sans wedding band, sits across from me. When he looks directly at me and says, *"Buon Natale,"* I realize his striking resemblance to Luke. His name is Mauro and he has a beautiful smile and speaks no English. For the occasion, he's worn a plaid Christmas sport coat I feel certain he only put on for this holiday. His hair is going from blonde to silver, and he's athletic and very fit. In fact, he turns out to be an ex downhill ski racer who now instructs and races bikes. He's fifty-five years old, Luke's exact age, divorced without children and grew up in the north of Italy. We chat easily and I'm happy to have three handsome men to take me away from my pity party. I'm also grateful to have a Luke look-a-like to be with on this lonely Christmas Eve.

After dinner the married men leave to join their families and Mauro invites me to join him in the bar for the evening's festivities.

Gratefully, the children are all taken away after Santa's visit, but I don't remember any other specifics about our time in the bar because of the complimentary shots of something I must have liked. I vaguely recall Mauro being a very uninhibited dancer and we danced, laughed and drank until they closed the bar and it was obvious we would leave together.

"Your room is closer," he whispers in my ear as he wraps an arm around my waist.

"Oh my, what big hands you have," I think.

The door has barely closed behind us before he pins me against the wall and kisses me; a long slow deep kiss with his athlete's body pressed perfectly against mine. Wow! I haven't been kissed like this in a long, long time. The next moment we fall onto the couch like teenagers, peeling each other's clothes off. When he pulls my t-shirt over my head, revealing my white lacy half bra (that I'm grateful I'd worn) he pauses appreciatively and says, "*bellissima.*"

I smile up at him and say, "*Buon Natale*," and then he shows me my present. Wow again. My jaw drops.

He is huge and so wide at the bottom I have to wrap two hands around him. He has a perfect athlete's body with extremely muscular legs and he's an experienced, generous lover who understands what a woman needs and wants and dives right in. He carries me into the bedroom where we proceed to get so wild we fall off the bed. I scream when my knee hits the floor and the people in the next room bang on the wall, making us laugh even louder, not deterring us from our endeavor. I have not had drunk sex in many, many years, and I know I was drunk because the next day I woke up without regrets, despite a badly bruised and scraped knee and shin. It had been a merry fucking Christmas after all.

The next day, Christmas Day, Mauro picks me up at one and drives me through the mountains to a small, "gingerbread" chalet restaurant where we spend three hours dining on a delicious ten-course Christmas feast! Several different wines accompany the food and dusk is just beginning to fall as we drive back to Sestriere. The sky is too beautiful to go inside so we settle into outside chairs next to an open fire pit at the foot of the ski slopes and drink prosecco as the stars begin to emerge. We end the evening with lovely sex and I thank him for being the best Christmas present I received that year. I will be leaving early the next morning for Luxembourg, and the rest of my adventure, happy to have shared two comfortably intimate days with a very capable man.

CHAPTER 18
A NEW YEAR IN LUXEMBOURG

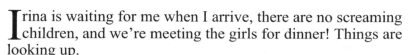

Irina is waiting for me when I arrive, there are no screaming children, and we're meeting the girls for dinner! Things are looking up.

Going from the very basic all-inclusive resort without snow, coffee, Internet, good food or nightlife to Luxembourg is like being bumped up from economy to first class. It's also a gift to spend time with my English-speaking, highly intelligent, beautiful young friends and I'll even take a Pilates class.

The next night, Irina has made a reservation for five of us girls at Café Belair, a small restaurant that serves an entire menu of gourmet hamburgers. The place is tiny, with eight tables and a bar that seats four. She had mentioned a handsome proprietor, but nothing could have prepared me for Pierre. Picture a bearded young red-haired Pierce Brosnan with brown eyes and a smile that could stop a train. And if that's not enough, he is gracious, charming and one of the most charismatic men I've ever met. We are all instantly smitten, and he must be accustomed to women reacting to him in this way as it neither emboldens nor ruffles him. In fact, he handles our open adoration with compassion, as if understanding our plight in being powerless to resist him. He is especially attentive to us all evening, making sure all our needs are met. (Well, not all.) He is married, and never acts inappropriately or flirtatiously, but he has a knack for making each of us feel as if we're the most important woman in the room. The only other man I've ever known with this ability is Warren Beatty.

The hamburger is also the best I've ever eaten, and I love burgers. It's a local, organic beef patty medium rare that comes perfectly cooked on a house-made bun that is chewy, crunchy and light, with a creamy black truffle and porcini mushroom spread, caramelized onions and a local melted cheese. When we all decline dessert, Pierre invites us to sample some of his impressive "brown liquors," asking each of us our preferences. He brings seven bottles to the table with shot glasses, sitting down to help us sample them all. Afterward, he asks each of us which we prefer, and I confess I prefer tequila or vodka.

"I am sorry I have no tequilas," he replies thoughtfully. "However, I have a vodka you might like."

He leaves and returns with a beautiful square crystal bottle. Holding it up to see how much is left, he says apologetically, "There's only a sip, but enough for you to try."

It's smooth and delicious. "That's very different, what gives it the amber color?" I ask.

"It's aged in oak," he replies, turning the bottle so the name is visible. *Woodka*.

"I'm sorry there's so little but please finish the rest," he says, emptying the bottle into my glass.

I look at the beautiful empty bottle and say, "This would be lovely for my limoncello."

"You *make* limoncello?" he asks.

"I do. Do you like it?"

"Not really," he says. "I find it too sweet."

"It's usually too sweet for me too, that's why I make my own...less sweet."

"I'd like to try that," he says.

"Then I'll make some and fill this bottle for you," I reply. He thanks me graciously and then formally introduces himself, asking my name. I reply, "I'm Zizi," and then instantly realize my embarrassing mistake. I turn bright red and cover my face with my hands, wishing I could disappear as my friends burst into hysterical laughter. My nickname, "Zizi" means "little penis" in French, which Irina had warned me about the moment I arrived in French-speaking Luxembourg. But my embarrassing faux pas leads to an entire conversation about my actual name, Zisela, from which Zia or Zizi is derived. "It's like Gisela with a Z," I explain, to which Pierre replies it's a version of the French Giselle. In his mouth that name sounds like the most beautiful name on earth and I wish it was mine. I also wish he was single and that I was twenty years younger and spoke French. He appears to be everything I want in a man. Irina and all the others agree.

Later that night, lying in bed, I replay the delightful evening and examine my feelings. What was it about him that had me instantly smitten? Of course, he's handsome, intelligent, charming and charismatic. He also fed me well and that's high on my list. Certainly, it's easy to be infatuated by all of those things. But I realize I have fallen in love with *how I felt in his presence.* This realization is key because it's exactly what I miss about Luke; how I felt with him, how his presence made me feel: loved, safe, passionate, appreciated and seen. How had a total stranger elicited those feelings in me? Do we have the ability to recognize a person capable of providing such things? Had *I* grown into someone able to recognize trustworthiness rather than a woman who attracts untrustworthy men? If indeed I had that ability, was I ready to attract a good man into my life? I remembered the handsome American man in the hotel bar in Athens. Was this another sign to show me what was possible? I believe it is and become so excited by the possibility I can hardly sleep. I finally drift off with the thought of staying open to meeting someone appropriate. I'm beginning to sense what that might that be like.

The following day, Irina takes me shopping to buy everything I need to make the limoncello. It will take one month to cure the lemon peels in the vodka, and then another year for the finished product to properly age. Irina will need to strain the lemon peels in thirty days, add the simple syrup and let the concoction sit until I arrive in March to finish the process. I am happy to be making something to give to Pierre, who unknowingly has provided me with such an important insight.

* * *

Marc's New Year's Eve party is wonderful, with about fifteen friends in his elegant downtown apartment. Two electric keyboards, microphones and speakers are set up in the living room, and four of us take turns singing all night. Everything is delicious, and my bacon-wrapped dates stuffed with almonds are a big hit. Everyone is elegantly dressed and the champagne (not Prosecco) flows like water. We watch the city's fireworks display from the living room windows, then stumble home sometime around two or three. It's a great way to bring in the New Year.

Spending the first week of the New Year with Irina is healing for me after such a (mostly) miserable week in the Alps. Three things help to alleviate my sadness in leaving her: Italian lessons, tango and knowing that I'll be returning to Luxembourg in March for an Eros Ramazzotti concert on my birthday! Irina feels like family.

On January fourth, I'm back in Cagliari, and take a tango lesson from Tonio. When he leaves, I binge-watch three episodes of *Masters of Sex* that is oddly pertinent to my life at the moment; in Virginia Johnson's new relationship she finally feels something instead of just having sex. Of course, it's exactly what I'm yearning for at the moment; sex with love and passion that is reciprocated.

I'm feeling trapped in my apartment in Castello while it's rainy and windy outside, without a car to escape in, a movie to pop into, or even a friendly bar. I won't go back to Vin Voglio (the only bar in Castello) because the owner sent me another early morning text message saying, *"Sempre un piacere,"* (I always think of you). Really? "Always" seems to be between 2 and 3 a.m. and there's no need to wonder exactly what he's thinking. I am not interested in a booty call any more, especially from a man with a sexy, bad boy vibe, as I have sworn off bad boys.

I now wish I'd rented a more centrally-located apartment, as it's too much effort to walk down and up the mountain in bad weather. I text Lili, asking if she's willing to brave the elements to come get "stunk and droned" with me tonight, and am happy to bribe her by cooking dinner. I have some leftover roasted vegetables and made a quick sauce I call Leftover Salsa Puta.

* * *

Another cold, wet winter week passes in which I rarely leave my house, but it's finally time for me to make my tango debut! Tonio drives us to a dance studio near Piazza Republica for my first tango *practica*: a dance for intermediate students or beginners to practice. A beginner's class is ending as we arrive and as I watch the couples on the floor, I feel relieved; I'm more advanced than anyone I see.

We begin dancing and I feel great, even as I see my reflection moving in the mirrored walls. We dance for about a half hour and then Tonio leaves me so other men will invite me to dance. The first is an adequate dancer but not a clear leader. Another man invites me to dance and I feel moderately comfortable. As the *practica* ends, more experienced dancers arrive for the *milonga*, and I move to the sidelines to watch.

One woman is exceptionally good: I watch her feet and the way she maintains her balance, her backward leg extensions and the way her arm and hand rest gently on her partner's back, hoping the correct way to execute moves is being recorded in my brain. Another man invites me to dance and I explain that I'm a *principiante,* a beginner. He says not to worry but proves to be a confusing leader. I have no idea how to follow his lead and after we finish, retreat to the rest room.

I return and lean against the wall to watch the expert woman dancing with a man who stands out in both style and ability. He is also extremely handsome with wild, long curly salt and pepper hair, a deep tan and gorgeous smile. His unique style sets him apart, and I wonder what it would be like to dance with him. As soon as the thought enters my mind, I begin to feel scared, afraid I'm not good enough and decide to leave.

It's freezing out when I walk to Florio to meet Lili. Everyone's crowded into the bar because of the cold and I'm lucky to find two seats. Massimo, one of the owners, sits down next to me and introduces me to his friend, Davide, a chef. We have an interesting chat about the upscale restaurant where he works, and he invites me to stop by one day for lunch. By the time Lili arrives, thirty minutes later, a friend of Davide's has also arrived. Stefano speaks perfect English, and when he learns I'm from San Francisco, tells us a fascinating story about being held for questioning on suspicion of murder there fifteen years earlier. I remember the story from the news, because there are not many unsolved murders in that upscale neighborhood. He swears he did not do it, but who knows what to think?

Around ten, Lili and I leave for Is Fraddis, a tiny Sardinian restaurant across the street from my first apartment where I used to watch people dine from my balcony. It is intimate and cozy, not the kind of place I'd feel comfortable dining alone, and Tonio says it's too expensive for him. Lili and I have a wonderful dinner while I flirt with a handsome (married) man sitting directly across from me with his wife. The open attention of married men here always surprises me, but none of them has ever made a move in any way. It makes me wonder if Italian marriages are more open to infidelities than ours or if the myth of Italian men having mistresses is true. It seems to be in other parts of Italy but from what I've seen, does not seem to be the case in Cagliari.

The next day, when Tonio calls to see how I fared at the *milonga*, I tell him about the incredibly good dancer I saw. When he asks me to describe him, he laughs and says, "Of course, that's Gabby, the best dancer on the island!" Then to my amazement he adds, "He has never taken a lesson, but I think he lived in Buenos Aires for a while."

Secretly I wish to dance with him but don't mention this to Tonio.

CHAPTER 19

NO MORE WALKS IN THE WOOD

—— ✦✦◆✦✦ ——

Glenn Frey died yesterday, January 18th, in New York at the age of 67 and, despite the fact that I hadn't seen him in ten years, it hit me hard. We met in the spring of 1970 when he was twenty-one and newly arrived in L.A. with his singing partner, JD Souther, who became my lover. They became an integral part of the scene I was in from then on, and we hung out and played at the Troubadour on Santa Monica Boulevard with up-and coming-singer/songwriters like Linda Ronstadt, Jackson Browne and the Flying Burrito Brothers. Steve Martin, the Smothers Brothers and Cheech and Chong were regulars, while Billy Joel and Elton John debuted there. We did too many drugs, stayed up all night singing, listening, writing, laughing, drinking and eating at Dan Tana's down the block. I was still in the Hollywood cast of *Hair* in '70 and '71 and would go there after my show ended at midnight. It was an innocent time because we were all so young and hopeful. Glenn had big dreams, as did many of us, but he seemed more serious and more dedicated than the rest of us. He always liked to say that JD "snagged all the girls" (which was mostly true), but that activity took a lot of time and focus from his career, while Glenn dedicated himself to the fulfillment of his biggest ambition.

His death has thrown me into a serious funk. He played a small but unforgettable role in the best time in my life, and it's disappearing. The music and harmonies Glenn created in The Eagles are on a level of their own; musical magic that only happens when there's an intimate connection between artists and a common dedication to the perfection of their sound. Glenn had a bumpy ride but always landed in the right place, and after all, none of us gets out alive. *No More Walks in the Wood* will haunt me in a different way now.

Two days later the malaise dissipates, and I make myself walk down the mountain to the *supermarcato*, to load up on a week's worth of groceries. Just as music has been therapy on this trip, so is cooking. It now serves as a form of meditation and a form of service. I pay attention when I'm slicing and dicing, and then I'm able to nourish other people with my creations. I buy a haunch of pork to slow roast North Carolina style and invite Rinaldo to join me for lunch the next day, Friday, and Lili for dinner on Saturday. After a hilarious ten-minute FaceTime call with Rinaldo, he says, in Italian, "It's incredible how much we make each other laugh when I speak no English and you only speak a little Italian. Imagine if we understood each other perfectly!" It's true. No one here makes me laugh as much as he does.

This morning, my teacher Isa, is meeting me at the Vodafone store to help me sort out the ridiculous monthly cell phone debacle of paying over and over again for charges that are never clear. Coincidentally, the restaurant where the handsome chef Davide works is only one block away so, we plan to go for lunch. By now, I'm feeling a lot better.

It's a good thing Isa went with me to the Vodafone store to sort out my account as the man behind the counter (in Isa's words) was *molto brutto*, (not very nice). We didn't get very far after thirty minutes of discussion, leading to an unbelievable – if typically – Italian bottom line: I have to pay separately at different times of the month for three different phone services: international calling, SMS messages and Internet. The total adds up to 23 euro, which is incredibly cheap. However, I must pay ten euro on the fourteenth of the month and fifteen on the twenty fourth. I can only pay in increments of five. I would never have believed this without Isa's fluent Italian, and it epitomizes the lack of sense, organization, reason, or forethought that pervades many aspects of Italian life. I had no idea how well-organized America was until I lived in Italy.

After the thirty-minute argument at Vodafone, we walk one block to Cucina Eat, Davide's restaurant. When we enter, he greets me with "Ciao, Zizi" and comes out from behind the bar to give me cheek kisses. When I introduce Isa as my friend and teacher, he congratulates her for doing such a good job. He thinks I speak Italian really well, which is a pleasant revelation! A week later, I return for lunch, notice that half of Davide's eyebrows are missing and ask if he'd gotten burned. "No," he says, shaking his head, "nerves." I must have looked perplexed, because he reaches up and plucks out some eyebrow hairs to demonstrate. It makes me wonder how and why Sardinian men (Davide, Rinaldo, Tonio, my landlord) are such nervous wrecks? The level of stress here is so much less than America, it feels like a mystery.

Tango lessons are going well and tonight Tonio takes me to a *practica* very close to my house in Castello. It's an ethereal grotto-like space in an ancient building, just below street level. The original "herringbone style" stone arched ceiling has been restored and the whole room is lit by candlelight. I feel uncomfortable in the crowd of people who all knew one another when a man approaches and asks me to dance. He's a good leader and I'm able to follow well enough to dance a whole *tanda* or set of three songs. I am proud of myself when another man asks me to dance, and I know I'm getting the hang of it and becoming less fearful.

The following week, Tonio tells me it's time for me to take some "women's technique" classes with a female teacher. Two days later, I walk thirty-five minutes to the outskirts of the city to Karen Salevsky's dance studio. She's a tiny beautiful woman with green eyes and red hair who speaks only a little English. On the walls are stunning photos of her dancing with her husband and partner, a handsome Argentinean named Luis Signoretti. The studio is large enough to hold about fifty dancers, with an old wooden floor, mirrors on the walls, and ballet bars along one wall that make me feel at home. She partners me (taking the man's role) to determine my level of ability, and immediately begins to teach me. Within minutes, she has shown me how to adjust simple mistakes of position and balance that instantly change my perspective on dancing. It's like a miracle to me. Why hadn't I done this sooner? It makes perfect sense that a woman's perspective as a follower will be different than a man's and by the end of the hour, I've graduated to another level of expertise, and ask how often I can come. I want to learn as much as possible with her in the two months I have left. I agree to private lessons twice a week (at $25 euro), and an intermediate class (5 euro) twice a week. There are also *practicas* and *milongas* on different nights, and I'm very excited.

* * *

Last night I met Christina for her "maybe it's not really a goodbye party" (again). I think this is number three. She is like the runaway bride. The following day, she texts to say she'll be staying, and as of this morning, she's leaving for Rome. It's hard to follow, but I understand completely how difficult it is to break away from an emotionally satisfying relationship even when you know it's doomed. (I say "doomed" only because she is definitely returning stateside next month to help her sister with her first baby, and also because her *fidanzato,* boyfriend, has a young son whom he would never leave.) She doesn't want to live in Cagliari forever and he won't leave, so it's difficult to imagine any other scenario than it being ultimately doomed.

Their situation recalls my own with Luke in the sense that we came to a point, after five years, where we needed different things. I think our sixteen-year age difference played a significant role, as I entered the last phase of my life while he was still in his prime at fifty-four. There were things I wanted to do while I still could, the most important being travel and an opportunity to live in Italy. Even though I believed it was the right choice, separation was physically and emotionally difficult. It took eight months to feel okay when I got into bed at night. I still miss him, still want him wrapped around me, but it no longer makes me cry, which I take as progress. For the first six months I felt like one of the walking wounded, but now I see the wisdom of the old adage, "Time heals everything."

CHAPTER 20
WINTER DRAGS ON
◆◆◆◆◆

Everyone in Sardinia is beginning to look the same to me; men and women with short black hair (natural or dyed), scarves wrapped around their necks and black clothing. Most men have black beards, thick black eyebrows waxed into shape, shaved heads if they are balding or else dyed black. As a woman who loves men with silver hair, I am continually disappointed. They wear black stocking caps with a strange looking empty pouch in the back that may hark back to traditional Sardinian garb. They are an interchangeable population that I believe reflects how provincial and "same" they are in their thinking. I find it suffocating, predictable, and boring, so I book a long weekend in Rome to visit Christina, who now lives there.

She recently introduced me to InterNations, an online international social networking group with chapters all over the world, except of course, in Cagliari. We've signed up to attend an *apricena* (appetizers and wine) event at a high-end hotel/shopping complex Saturday night. The group in Rome appears to offer exactly what I'm craving: global diversity, and the possibility of cosmopolitan age-appropriate multi-lingual men.

Very loud drums begin again, because today is Carnivale, the last big party before lent begins. I am not talking about one set of drums, but an orchestra of kettledrums. I've heard them on two different nights, the first time until after one in the morning from the rooftop where they practice one block from my house.

I open my door to see twenty drummers wearing clownish costumes march by, followed by about fifty people, many of whom are dressed as pirates and nuns with garish makeup. I understand the significance of pirates, but nuns with makeup? Fallen women? I shoot a short video that I'll post on Facebook and feel that my job for the day is now complete.

Lili comes up for an early dinner and we walk down to the street for a "swing ball" where the actor, Roberto Boassa, is flinging himself around enthusiastically. I love being with him because he's so interested in everything and so *alive*. He is the only Sardinian I've met who lives life voraciously and this attitude is one of the things I dearly miss.

In advance of my trip to Rome in four days, I've received "twinkles" (text messages) from five InterNations members, one of whom looks lovely and is named Rocco...be still my heart. Our text flirtation continues throughout the day, until I check his profile and see that like every man I've met this year, he's 41 years old. Three others have "twinkled" me since yesterday so, maybe it will be interesting and, if nothing else, refreshing to meet new people and experience a change of environment. It is also Chinese New Year and I find a Chinese restaurant in Rome on line!

The highlights of my Roman holiday are: The Roman delicacy, *Carciofi fritti* – an entire artichoke flash fried to a dark brown and looking inedible, that crunches and disappears instantly – discovering that when it rains the river rises and floods the ancient Roman sewers, The Priscilla catacombs (the oldest in Rome dating back to the first century AD), The Leonardo Da Vinci Museum of Inventions and the gardens of The Villa d'Este. The InterNations event is disappointing but

I don't care because just being in the living ancient history that is Rome is a magnificent experience.

CHAPTER 21
THE END OF BOREDOM

By the end of February, I've finally found some cultural diversity in Cagliari courtesy of the elegant and intimate jazz club, Jazzino. The music has an international flair and continually changes while the food is some of the best nouvelle cuisine in Cagliari. The fixed price of twenty-five euro includes live music, a four-course dinner and a big glass of stellar house red! My favorite appetizer is a beet carpaccio with a dollop of goat cheese and sprinkle of pistachio nuts that I include in my recipes at www.notesfromabroad.biz. When Bill and Jessica return from Spain, it quickly becomes our favorite night spot.

I have a great time preparing another Mexican feast for Rinaldo, Bill and Jessica: nachos with a seasoned ground beef/pork combo, beans, Dolce Sardo cheese, jalapeños (that cost $8 in the tiny international market), and pico de gallo, slow-cooked pentola beans with bacon, peppers, onions, garlic and tomatoes, and chicken quesadillas topped with rajas and crema. Since corn tortillas do not exist on Sardinia, I use a classic Sardinian chip called Gutiau that everyone loves. Roberto Boassa joins us for coffee with his smoldering excitement that comes out in bursts of laughter and animation and reminds us of Roberto Benigni.

My daughter Ariane's fiftieth birthday arrives in less than a week, and it's hard to wrap my head around this number, despite the fact that I can barely remember my life without her. I was only twenty when she was born, so she's been with me for the major portion of my life. Essentially, we grew up together. It's very hard not being with her to celebrate and so far, her gifts, that I mailed a month ago, have yet to arrive.

Other disappointments are also piling up: I've received a rejection for a writer's residency in Sienna, my new prescription glasses do not arrive as promised and then arrive broken, Rinaldo's proposed concert plan for us falls through, and I still have no idea where I'll go when I return to the states in September. My own birthday is a week away and I don't feel celebratory. I even had an hour-long meditation yesterday without the usual uplifting effect. I am tired of being alone in my apartment because it's too cold, windy and damp to walk around the city, and I'm indulging in frequent pity parties.

* * *

Thankfully, the next day Ariane's gifts arrive, and Bill and Jess go to Jazzino with me to see a tango quartet, Novafonic! I feel surrounded by beauty which always makes me happy; the four musicians are stunningly handsome and the music sounds like a sexy, jazzy version of the soundtrack from *Last Tango in Paris* with a modern twist. These diversions with friends help to alleviate my on-going malaise and fend off depression.

I hate being "cooped up" in the Castello in winter, and just want it to end: I'm so very tired of grey stones and grey skies without any green spaces. It throws me way out of synch with nature and the natural rhythm of things, and I'm not certain how to counteract the effects. I'm having a harder and harder time concentrating and focusing, even with guided meditations. I feel very discouraged, out of balance, off kilter, and disconnected. It's time to pull up my big girl panties.

I spend the next five days listening to guided meditations, practicing Vipassana meditation and Yoga, and finally climb out of the hole I had dug for myself. What lesson do I learn? When I recognize the signs of being disconnected and unable to get outside in nature to ground myself, I go inside. Sometimes, I just need to grovel in the dirt before I remember that I have access to this amazing internal space. Filled with gratitude, I shift out of my doldrums just in time for my birthday. Life is good again.

Happy birthday to me! The sun is shining when I wake up...my first birthday gift. I make myself a cappuccino, shower, dress, and walk down the hill to have my hair done. When Alessandra asks what I want, I tell her "something young" because it's my birthday. When she asks how many years, I receive a startled squeal and jaw drop from her, the young male hairdresser and another customer. It's a perfect ego boost birthday present. Lili meets me and takes a photo of my new hairdo to post on Facebook then takes me to Sushi Tao for a birthday lunch of Thai coconut soup and a teriyaki bento box. She presents me with a tiny bud and pipe along with a beautiful handmade card and a heart shaped lactose-free orange and chocolate cake! She has also brought my new prescription sunglasses that aren't much good in the sun but look fabulous...(perfectly typical Italian design).

Later, I settle into my couch to read birthday greetings from around the world and Ari texts asking if I've received any deliveries. My family sent flowers, which hadn't arrived, but the thought brings tears to my eyes. I put on a new dress with new long rhinestone earrings and call a taxi (as there are hurricane force winds blowing) to meet Bill and Jess at Jazzino.

We polish off an assortment of appetizers and a bottle of bubbly, and as the band takes the stage, I recognize the singer, Francesca Corrias, who I've seen many times, singing perfectly in English, Italian, Spanish, and now Portuguese. It's impossible to sit still to Brazilian music, so we dance around in our chairs. Bill and I are still hungry, and all they have left is lasagna. We agree to split one portion with a bottle of red. It is the first disappointing food we've tasted there; old and reheated. Were I not so hungry, I would have passed. When the band finishes, we order a round of *mirto* and as usual, are the last customers to leave.

The winds are still whipping around when we leave, and Bill says he'd clocked them at sixty knots on the boat earlier and felt seasick all afternoon. The taxi drops me off at my front door, and then continues down the hill to deliver Bill and Jess to their boat in the marina.

It was a wonderful birthday evening and I'm happy to fall into bed at one thirty. I decide to take half an Ambien because I don't want the alcohol to wake me in the middle of the night when my blood sugar drops, crawl into bed and immediately fall asleep.

I have no idea how long I slept before waking up, feeling sick; the old lasagna wants to leave my body. I walk to the toilet to throw up; a rarity for me as I never get sick. Thankfully, it's over quickly, and I brush my teeth before going back to bed.

The next morning, lying peacefully asleep on my back, I hear a very loud gurgling sound that penetrates my earplugs. Thinking I'm dreaming, I doze off only to be awakened again by the same sound. I take out one earplug to listen, and then, I smell it: sewage. My eyes fly open, I sit up and my feet hit the floor into two inches of cold water. I tiptoe two steps to turn on the lights to see that the entire apartment is flooded. The stench is unmistakable, and I see sludgy water bubbling up through the shower drain. Grabbing my cell, I text the landlord, who immediately replies, promising to call someone to come over. I grab a towel, dry my feet and put on my Uggs, scrambling around the apartment picking up everything on the floor: my shoes and boots, a big empty suitcase, the bag with my tango shoes, and a portable heater. I place it all on a folded towel on the couch, pack a small overnight bag and wait outside the front door, as the smell is too foul.

Two hours later, a couple of men arrive and pull the cover off the sewer drain directly in front of my front door. Thick brown sludge hovers menacingly at the top. One of the men inserts a long, wood-handled instrument that looks like a garden tool, moving it around. "It's clogged," he says in Italian. Obviously, I think and then wonder if it was the lasagna. After fifteen minutes of coaxing and stirring to free the drain, one of the men begins flushing the toilet. When it flushes properly, and the drain is cleared, they replace the lid and leave.

The closest B&B is one block away and I secure a room for the night, then walk around the corner to a cafe for a much-needed cappuccino and *cornetto*. By the time I finish, Marisa, my housekeeper, has arrived to clean. She gives me a disgusted look and says, *E brutto*! (it's ugly), then shrugs her shoulders and tells me not to worry. I roll my little suitcase up the street and check into a cute one-bedroom suite that is freezing cold with only one small radiator. I walk back to my house and grab the portable heater only to discover that the plug does not fit any of the outlets in my room. Luckily, the hostess provides me with an adapter.

Later that night, when I walk down to check on my apartment, both French windows are propped open and the ceiling fan is on. I light an apple pie-scented candle that Bill and Jessica gave me for my birthday, leaving it burning on the kitchen sink and by the next morning, my house just smells like apple pie. It also feels like the first day of spring, and I enjoy a short respite for the next few days until the ninth of March when I get an email telling me that another old dear friend has died. Three days later an even closer friend passes. Both were only one year older than I, and this hits me hard on many levels.

As I have never found acceptable answers to the question of death and grief in the conscious world, I dive deeply into meditation to deal with the loss. As a result, during the following days, I replace the sorrow with gratitude and am reminded how much there is to be grateful for: my wonderful daughter and grandchildren, my incredibly good health and youthful appearance, the ability to understand and adapt, an appreciation of a wide range of marvels from food and architecture to nature, my talents, sense of humor and most of all, an ability to love on so many levels. I feel excited about life's possibilities again like a child on Christmas Eve, going to bed too excited to sleep, knowing the morning will hold treasure. How lucky am I to be living this dream? Once again, I climb out of the depths of grief into the heights of gratitude.

CHAPTER 22

A POSSIBLE CHANGE OF HEART

— ❖❖❖❖ —

As I walked to the tango studio this morning, a car pulled alongside me and tooted the horn. I glanced sideways, saw it was a lone man, and kept walking. A few yards later, he rolled down the window and called my name. It was Rinaldo, laughing uncontrollably because he knew I thought he was a stranger trying to pick me up. The neighborhood near the school is Cagliari's "red light district" so, I thought the driver mistook me for a "working girl" (*putana*). I got in and we laughed all the way to the studio.

I love my new tango teachers, Karen and Luis, who teach more of a modern style of Argentine tango than the one I've learned from Tonio. Today, at my second lesson, Karen says I'm ready to dance at a *milonga* although I don't feel ready. She assures me that going forward, much of my learning will happen while I'm dancing.

My first tango lesson with Luis, Karen's Argentinean husband, is transformational! He suggests I make several simple adjustments that, when mastered, will make me an excellent dancer. Dancing suddenly feels easier and more natural to me and I wish I'd met them sooner as I only have five weeks left to study.

However, my immediate future is uncertain and it's making me feel nervous. I've spent a year taking notes and journaling with the intention of putting the book together somewhere in Europe before returning to the states. With that in mind, I applied to three writers' residencies and a second rejection arrived via email today, leaving only one more possibility in Spain. If that falls through, I'll need to figure out a whole new plan to find an environment conducive to writing. I have "woven" a lot of material and now need to "sew the suit." I think about revisiting Ikaria, or an inexpensive spot somewhere in Italy, and decide it's time to reach out to friends.

* * *

Today begins brilliantly with a decision to face it anew, following my morning meditation. The phrase "fake it till you make it" pops into my head and I welcome the day with enthusiasm and wonder, expecting the unexpected. Buoyed by bright sunshine and my positive attitude, I dress for spring with subtle sex appeal in faded jeans and a soft white, tailored men's shirt with an expensive lacy French bra beneath it. I prefer *feeling* sexy rather than dressing sexy. The day is warm with a bright blue sky as I walk down the mountain to Piazza San Benedetto for Rinaldo's "*Suono al civico*" concert. Lili will be meeting me, so I order a cappuccino at Florio and take two of the last seats at a table in the shade with a clear view of the balcony where the singer will perform. The piazza is already filled with hundreds of people, many of whom I know.

As soon as I sit down, Lili arrives, bubbling over with her usual enthusiasm and Tonio texts asking if I'm there. A minute later, he comes over to invite me to a 7 p.m. tango *practica* in Castello very near my house. When he leaves Lili says quietly to me, "Tell me you haven't revisited that please," to which I say, "Nope. Not going there again. Waiting for what I really want."

The wonderful mezzo soprano who'd sung at Christmas walks onto the balcony and begins to sing. What could be better than Italian opera in a tiny piazza in Italy on a glorious Sunday morning in the spring? We order Campari spritzes to celebrate and let the heavenly arias fill us with joy and wash away our sins. I love being enveloped in music and filled with gratitude for this magical place and my dear friend, Lili. I am lightyears away from California but feel perfectly at home.

Afterwards, Rinaldo has too many commitments to join us, so Lili and I walk down to the marina to sit in the sun and enjoy a light lunch at Locando Cadeo, my favorite place for foccacia bread open-face treats, which are always fresh and delicious. Later, we stroll up Via Roma to sip a caffé in one of Cagliari's most elegant bars, Svitzero. Since it's Sunday, we conclude our progressive meal by walking two blocks up to Piazza Yenne, where we buy a vegan dessert at Coccodi to bring back to my place for later. The day feels positively celebratory and instead of walking up the mountain, we take the number eight bus up to Castello. When we get to my place, Lili sorts through the bag of clothes I'm gifting her before I leave, choosing a couple of things. In an attempt to fend off sadness, we watch two episodes of a British comedy called *Peep Show*, on YouTube and laugh ourselves silly.

I change into my tango clothes and Tonio knocks on my door at 6:45 to walk me the two blocks to the *practica*. The studio is the same one he'd taken me to in January, the grotto-like space below street level and like many places in the Castello, you would never know it exists. Lit solely by candles, the oval dance floor is exquisitely beautiful, with the low curved ceiling of herringbone brick. We watch the last fifteen minutes of a *milonga* style class, which is fast and complicated, and I wonder if I'll ever master that one. Standing against the wall with other women waiting to be invited to dance, I consider bailing, and then one of the very good dancers walks toward me, extending his hand. He speaks no English, but I explain in Italian that I'm a beginner, and he's very patient and courteous through three dances. I feel pretty good about my ability to follow him and more than a little nervous that Tonio is watching. When we finish dancing, he returns me to my spot against the wall and a few minutes later, the *best* dancer in the place asks me to dance. Bubbling over with nervous laughter, I thank him profusely and tell him that he's way too good of a dancer for me. He takes my hand and with a George Clooney smile tells me not to worry. He is the same incredible dancer I'd seen at my first *practica*, the one Tonio called "the best dancer on the island." He's also the best looking.

He tells me his name is Gabriele, but everyone calls him Gabby, and he speaks English fairly well. When he learns I'm from San Francisco, he tells me he visited two years ago and fell in love with it. This is incredible as very few Sardinians vacation in California; if they go to the states the destination is usually New York.

We dance a *tanda* (set) of four tangos and he's so easy and amazing to dance with that I relax enough to truly enjoy it. He makes me feel like a much better dancer than I am, and I love the way he holds me very close, which is no doubt why I become so upset.

After dancing with Gabriele, I tell Tonio I'm too upset to dance because two of my friends died this week. "What are you going to do now?" he asks. "Go home and cry," I reply. And that's exactly what I do: surrender to the deep sadness around the loss of two friends. On top of that, yesterday, I Face Timed with Luke for the first time in a year and burst into tears as soon as I saw his face. Luckily, the phone froze and gave me a few minutes to collect myself. Our year of separation and thousands of miles hasn't made any difference in my feelings and looking into his eyes again makes me cry. Am I still in love with him or with the love we shared? The loss of the love and friends we shared overwhelms me and I cannot sleep.

Once again, I find myself resorting to a sleeping pill to get through the night.

The following morning, I awake with interesting realizations. My "old self," i.e. old patterns, are beginning to shift and right now my ego is fighting for its life. That part of me is resisting the changes, craving the comfort of sameness, yet my old habits bring me nothing but grief and unhappiness. My ego seems to be attached to it – that's why I was so hard on Tonio, who likes to suffer! I have that same trait and I'm not so pleased with it. Amazing how our old attachments to being miserable hang on – even when we find ourselves in the midst of paradise.

* * *

But now the new is taking over. On this trip, I'm opening up in a different way. And today culminated with a huge win: dancing tango at a *practica* with the amazing Gabriele! Even more miraculously, he speaks English, has visited San Francisco, and now lives in Chia, one of the most beautiful beaches in Sardinia. He danced four tangos with me. He was very patient, generous with his knowledge of the dance, and we laughed when I made mistakes. I think I left after dancing with him because I wanted to exit on a high note and was afraid to sully that experience by dancing with someone else.

* * *

After deciding to focus on my successes rather than failures, I begin to feel amazed, delighted, encouraged, energized, inspired and renewed! For the last week, I've thought of the many outrageous moments when I manifested something wonderful that I really wanted. Years ago, I saw a magazine photo of an Art Deco diamond and emerald bracelet set in platinum and worth about $7500. Three hours later I found that same piece at a yard sale for $10. Once I spied a journalist's photo next to his byline in the *San Francisco Chronicle* and thought, "Now there's a man I'd like to be with," then he walked into a party at my house a week later. I dreamt about many things that later happened – like being cast in *Hair*, living with my boyfriend in a house on the lake. The ability to create what I want has been with me all my life and now I'm learning how to dispel all the things that stand in the way. An interesting word *dispel*. Yes, let's take away the power of negative thinking, end the spell, undo the spell. Magic is real, and I feel excited about my future once again.

* * *

I embarked on this journey a year ago with trepidation, beneath my bravado. A friend once said, if you want to know what a person is hiding, imagine the opposite of how they present themselves to the world. Everyone thinks of me as the bravest woman they know, but "bravery" was how I hid my fear, even from myself. What was I doing going off alone on a European adventure without a plan? I know much of my fear is left over from a damaged childhood, (a topic to be explored in a different book), but right now I know one thing. I am moving on and the past is not invited. I'm ready to commit to everything that nourishes me, from travel, to new food, new friends, and new love.

* * *

Excited about going to Sicily, I search Google for hotels, beaches, hot springs and rental cars then make myself dinner. I take my trash to the bins at the end of my street and meet my young neighbor, Fabrizio. We sometimes run into one another at Vin Voglio and only know each other casually. He speaks no English, so our conversations have been limited to a very basic Italian. All I know about him is that he's thirty-eight and separated with a two-year-old son he sees on weekends.

"Ciao Zizi, I thought you had disappeared. Where have you been and why didn't you call me like you said you would?" he asks, smiling broadly. We kiss lightly on cheeks, as all Italians do in greeting, and stand in his doorway chatting. After explaining that I've been traveling quite a lot, I say I need to get home to do some writing. Before I know what's happening, he leans forward and kisses me on the lips. I immediately pull away, wipe my lips, and ask if he's crazy.

"*No, no, un altro,*" he begs. "Kiss me again."

"Fabrizio," I say sternly, "do you have any idea how old I am?" When I tell him, I think he might faint. He spends a full minute wide-eyed and sputtering. "How is this possible?" he asks. "This must be some kind of magic! What drugs do you take? I don't believe it!" I add a log to the fire by telling him my daughter is older than he is, and then make my exit, quickly walking up the street to my house. As soon as I get inside, the text bell rings on my phone. His text message begins with "*Amore mio,*" (my love) and continues with a plea to "once again feel your soft hot lips for just one moment." He describes the "torture" I'm submitting him to. How could he ever "forget the feel of my lips?" He "would be unable to sleep without another kiss." I have to call Lili to translate the word "torture," to which she replies, "What kind of spell did you put on him or is he just insane?"

"Well," I respond, "It's my own fault. I've been getting clearer about how I want to feel with a man and how I want him to feel about me and this is kind of what I asked for, but not this distorted and not with him!" I remember Joe Dispenza saying that the universe has an incredible sense of humor. Copy that.

What follows is the text conversation that took place over the next thirty minutes.

Fabrizio: Why do you go away?

Z: To see Sicily and meet friends in Toscana and also to finish the book I'm writing at a writer's residency in Spain.

F: I was talking about now. Will you come to me to watch a film with me and stay a little while together?

Z: It's not possible because I'm writing now.

F: Zizi, your lips are hot.

Z: You're making me laugh.

F: I wish I could have them again even just for a little while. Come for just a moment...one last kiss tonight.

Z: No, no, no, no. I'm sorry.

F: You don't want me? Say you do...

Z: Not like that.

F: How then?

Z: Good night Fabri.

F: How cold.

Z: I'm sorry but I need to write now.

F: Say something nice to me.

Z: You are very sweet.

F: If you change your mind, will you write to me tonight? Will we see each other for a kiss? Promise me that. Even if it's late, if you want to, will you write me?

Z: I will be writing for many hours.

F: You could write for the whole night but, if you want me, even if just a kiss, I'll be awake. Can we see each other for a kiss? Only one and then you can go back to writing. I swear. One...

Lili finally dictates a phrase for me to text in Italian that politely explains that I find his advances offensive. He responds with profuse apologies and I'm left wondering what might be wrong with these men? Are they sex-starved, over-sexed, immature, hopelessly romantic, delusional or all of the above? For the next month, I carefully avoided walking past his house and thankfully, never run into him again.

CHAPTER 23

LAST TANGO IN CAGLIARI

———— ♦♦♦♦♦ ————

The sun came out this morning and stayed out all day – what a miracle. After living so many years in the temperate climate of San Francisco, I have a renewed appreciation for the glorious warmth of the sun on an early spring day after a real winter.

It's still warm as I walk to my first *milonga* at Karen and Luis's studio. For the first half hour, no one invites me to dance, which is both relieving and disappointing, as I'm still a very uncertain dancer. However, as soon as the first man dances with me, seven others follow, and I perform better than I'd thought I would. Feeling pleased with myself, I stand against one wall watching the one I really want to dance with moving effortlessly around the floor. Something about him sets off alarm bells in me; tells me I could fall in love with him and it could hurt me. I have not heard those bells in a long time. He falls into the "sexy ugly" category of men, with a rough face and harsh features, but his body and hands are beautiful and he's a fabulous dancer. I watch my friend Elisabeta, Rinaldo's ex-wife, dance with him and ask her later who he is. She isn't sure. What is it about him that's familiar and why is it so disconcerting? Another greatest love story that never happened? I change out of my tango shoes to signal the end of my availability and gladly accept when Elisabeta offers me a ride home. My progress in tango fills me with gratitude and I leave feeling good about the way I navigated through the evening.

As I wake up the following morning, I have an *astounding* realization: when I see photos of happy couples who have been married for a long time, I subconsciously think, "I'll never have that." Although it's true that I won't celebrate a forty or fifty-year wedding anniversary, it also feels like a self-fulfilling prophecy. I may never have that kind of longevity, but I can certainly have everything else a long happy relationship implies. It's amazing to me that the subconscious mind – always in the driver's seat – is so well concealed and subversive. I decide to reframe that subconscious thought in a positive way the next time I catch it. Instead of allowing it to sadden me, I'll remember that I can have all the things a long-term relationship brings – just for a shorter period of time. I may only have twenty years left, but why shouldn't I spend them with someone I love?

* * *

Tonight is the first night of the local "Skepto" film festival in Cagliari and it's surprisingly wonderful. As a long-time attendee of The Mill Valley, Telluride and San Francisco festivals, I wasn't certain what to expect. Lili, Bill, Jessica and I meet for lemon drops at Moonshine beforehand, then grab a bite to eat at the festival, catered by Luigi Pomata, one of Cagliari's most famous chefs. Everything is great: the food, the auditorium's plush red velvet seats and the films. When I climb the hill home at midnight, I feel very pleased and happy.

The next day, April fifteenth, is my first beach day this spring and it is glorious! Wearing my bikini under my jeans, I meet Roberto Boassa, the next big Italian movie star, at Sella Diavolo kiosk where we snag two sling beach chairs. He tells me that after our last meeting, when I told him I believed he was destined to become the next famous Italian character actor and to go for it if it's what he truly wanted, he got roles in two films; one small and the next bigger. He says he is now committed, and I have no doubt he will succeed: he is a "one of a kind" character and one day we will all see him on the big screen.

* * *

Fortunately, I'm feeling more excited than sad today, following a tough weekend I know is my last. Rinaldo's group is performing in the Suono al Civico concert on the balcony in Piazza San Domenico, across from Florio, and the first person I run into is Paola Ciabatti, my first friend on Sardinia! We haven't seen each other for several months because she works around the clock, and we both have tears in our eyes when we hug. I realize, later, that our entire conversation had been in Italian (because she speaks no English) and we really talked! I remember our early "conversations," relying on sign language and looking up every word in my dictionary. As we talk Giuseppe, who lives in the Piazza (and tried to help me find an apartment to rent last September), comes over for a hug, saying he heard I was leaving. I invite them both to my "Ciao Zizi" farewell party on Friday at Libarium.

There's an unusually large crowd, and the music begins just as I arrive, so I haven't had time to greet Rinaldo. With the sun directly in my eyes, I aim my phone camera at the balcony and take three shots without even trying to see. Later, zooming in on the first shot, Rinaldo is looking directly at me through a crowd of several hundred people. We have such a strong connection, and I keep thinking had we met another time, another place we might have become life partners (indeed, we may have been in another life).

At the very end of my morning guided meditation, I imagined myself being "showered with love." I felt sunlight pouring down, filling me with joy. Now, as the concert ends, I make my way to the balcony to put money into the donation basket and rose petals start falling on my head. Everyone gasps, breaking into wide grins, turning their faces up to be "showered with flowers." It's a magical moment and I savor it with tears in my eyes, before heading to Christina's fourth goodbye party at Isa's in Poetto.

At Isa's there are twelve people and enough food and wine for fifty. The homemade wine is the best I've had here. I've brought along a big bowl of my pico de gallo and brought *gutiau* for scooping (because they're better than the corn chips here that are on a par with Doritos). We sit outside eating and chatting for several hours until Omar, Christina's boyfriend, gives me a ride home. There is just enough time to shower and change for Sunday night tango in Castello, but when I get there, something odd happens. The earlier class is still in progress and several people stand on the edges of the studio to watch, so I do the same. The man I had seen at Karen's tango studio the week before, who had completely unnerved me, is there, and I have the same reaction.

My eyes fill with tears and I feel a constriction in my chest. I flee, knowing if he asks me to dance I'll fall apart. How can I explain or even comprehend the deep longing I feel for him, as though he is a lost love? I cry all the way home and for the next hour in my house. My emotions are on my sleeve these days because of the sadness of leaving, and I'm sure this plays a big part.

* * *

The next evening, as I get dressed for my last *milonga* in Cagliari, my good fortune fills me with gratitude. I had no idea whether or not tango would exist in Sardinia and I miraculously found several of the very best teachers within walking distance of my apartment. This past month has been mostly dedicated to tango and it's paid off handsomely. Checking my reflection in the mirror I approve of the simple black dress with the drop waist and flouncy skirt. "My last tango in Cagliari," I say aloud to my reflection, and smile.

* * *

As soon as I enter the grotto-like tango studio, I spot Gabby, who is dancing like Fred Astaire. "Well," I think to myself, "*Che sará*–whatever will be," and put on my tango shoes. As soon as they're fastened, a man approaches and invites me to dance. I smile and accept without explaining that I'm a beginner. We cruise the floor smoothly for three dances and he thanks me, leading me back to my seat. Several other men invite me to dance over the next half hour and I'm feeling extremely pleased with my progress. I wander into the entry area where the refreshments are set on a table and pour myself a small glass of wine, when a man's voice says, "Hello, San Francisco."

Turning around, I see Gabby's smiling face. "Would you like to dance?" he asks.

"Absolutely," I reply.

We move onto the dance floor and stand still in a Tango embrace for the space of one full breath in and out. We become one – melting into each other – breathing together with no thought, only simultaneous soft movement, out of our minds and into our bodies. Dancing with him is divine and effortless. At the end of the *tanda*, we stand at the edge of the dance floor, conversing. He tells me he lives in Chia, a beach town an hour's drive from Cagliari. I ask if he might consider teaching me privately, and he throws back his head and laughs. "I don't teach," he says, "and I never studied."

"Apparently, you didn't need to study. Just teach me what you know instinctively," I say.

"It's a long way to drive and I always make the trip just to dance," he explains.

"I live on the next street up," I say, "and have a large living room with a good floor for dancing. I took private lessons there last fall. You can even stay at my house. I have a couch that's very comfortable for me and you can have the bed."

He laughs again, placing his hand gently on my shoulder. "What an unusual proposal," he says with that perpetual smile that's so beautiful.

"Which part?" I ask, "the lessons or the bed?"

"Both," he says.

Now it's my turn to smile. "Seriously," I say. "Walk me home and I'll show you. I'm leaving in a few days and I'd love you to teach me, even if it's just once. I've never seen anyone dance like you and I've never felt as good dancing with anyone."

"Thank you," he says, "and I will at least walk you home."

On the way, we talk about his trip to San Francisco and New York the previous year and he tells me he'd spent two years in Buenos Aires dancing. When we enter my apartment, he says, "Yes, this is a perfect place for one couple to dance."

"And here is the bed I will gladly give up to you," I say, showing him the bedroom.

He regards me with amusement and gently moves my hair away from my eyes where it always falls. "Cara, I would prefer to share it," he says, allowing his hand to rest on my cheek.

My brain is too revved up to form thought. I'm captivated by his direct sincerity.

He holds my gaze, cocking his head slightly to one side, and asks, *"E tu?"*

My heart pounds in my throat. "I honestly didn't bring you here to seduce you," I say, hardly believing this is happening.

"What if I did?" he asks. "And you can have your lesson in the morning."

"OK but…" I take a long pause to choose how to tell him that I'll have sex with him, but I can't actually fall asleep with a man I'm not in love with. It's a safety issue for me that goes back to my damaged childhood. "I will *sleep* on the couch," I say.

Now he really laughs. "But look at this big bed. There is plenty of room for us both."

"It's difficult for me to sleep with anyone," I explain. "It's complicated."

"As you wish," he says, scooping me up into his arms.

He sits down on the bed, with me on his lap, and begins undressing me. It makes me feel like a little girl, and each time he uncovers an area, he kisses it: my neck, shoulders, arms, breasts and belly. He gently lays me on my back and removes my shoes, lightly kissing my feet, and up my legs, then slowly slides my panties off, placing kisses on all of the newly uncovered skin. "You are so beautiful," he says.

"So are you," I reply.

He has the deeply-tanned and muscular body of a surfer, his other passion besides tango, and approaches love making the same way he dances; slowly, gracefully and connected. In fact, we are "making love," not just having sex and I respond to his caresses and kisses like the starved being I have become. The more he gives, the more I want, and the more I respond, the deeper we go. Nothing like this has happened for me in a very long time; no one has loved me this way, and I feel totally safe. I am so spent when we finish, I fall asleep wrapped in his arms.

The sound of the espresso machine wakes me, and I realize it is morning and he's still with me. A moment later, he sits on the edge of the bed, holding a cup of coffee. "Do you like sweet?" he asks.

"Yes please," I reply.

"I thought so," he says, offering the cup and moving back to the kitchen. I prop myself up on pillows, pulling the duvet up over my breasts and smile to myself. I had slept in the same bed with a man. He comes back carrying his own cup and sits on the bed.

"Do you really leave in a few days?" he asks.

"In two actually," I reply.

"To San Francisco?" he asks.

"Not immediately. I'm going to Sicily for a month, then meeting up with a group of friends from California in Toscana for a month and then spending two months at a writer's retreat in Spain."

"You are a writer?"

"Yes."

"Brava! What do you write?"

"Books. I'm writing one about my year abroad now; my adventures in Italy."

He moves my hair away from my eye and lets his hand rest on my cheek. "I leave too," he says, "For Bali."

"To surf?" I ask.

"Yes, and maybe even tango. But at the moment, I must leave you very soon so, we have one hour more." He slowly peels the duvet off my chest. "Would you rather stay here in bed or dance?"

"That's an impossible choice to make," I say. "You choose."

* * *

I will let you, dear reader, decide how we spent our last hour together because either would have been orgasmic, but this encounter only exists in my imagination. Gabby is real as is everything I told you about him...everything that preceded my asking him to walk me home.

When I left the dance and went home alone, I was struck by how different Gabby seemed to be. He was a standout one-of-a-kind man in a society that did not encourage that, a well-traveled, English-speaking man, a charismatic individual in every sense of the word. His elegance on the dance floor came from a place of connectedness and sensuality and I began to imagine how he might be as a lover. Those thoughts led easily to what I had been missing, how I wanted to feel with a man, and how I wanted a man to feel about me. I invented a scene the way I wished it to play out so that I might be able to actually attract it in the future.

Being alone in a foreign land for eighteen months had forced me to delve more deeply into old issues and patterns that affected how I am in relationship. I uncovered deeper layers but hadn't yet found the love I craved from a partner. I had found it in friends, both male and female and more importantly, I'd learned what I don't want anymore. So, I made Gabby the perfect man to visualize. One who might come to me in real life, if I first allowed him in my dreams.

CHAPTER 24
ARRIVEDERCI CAGLIARI

—— ✦✦✦✦ ——

My last day in Cagliari I take my final tango lesson then walk up the hill to Libarium, the gorgeous outdoor bar/restaurant at the top of the Castello with a view of the west side of the island. Friends join me for my final "Ciao Zizi" party. Gerardo, my local grocer, presents me with one of his favorite CDs and some bottled water for the trip. His cousin Tony walks towards me with a big smile and says, "You are leaving," with such a somber face. More hugs, kisses and tears that make me feel as if I'm leaving "home" – a pleasant reminder that everyone I've come into contact with here has been extraordinarily kind and generous.

* * *

Back in my apartment, I organize my luggage with the knowledge that my suitcase is way over the weight limit of twenty kilos. I cannot lift it off the floor and have no idea how Paola and I will get it into her car.

I have two hours before we set off for the airport, so I head over to Bar Florio and Rinaldo's concert that celebrates Tango. Everyone is in costume for the theme of 1920 Buenos Aires. Irma, a round older woman, is wearing a 1920's bathing suit and carrying a parasol! The dancers emerge from the crowd into the piazza that is now a dance floor. All the local tango teachers are in costume, and it's magical: I cannot imagine a more fitting send-off.

Tonio is uncomfortable, as the woman he pines for is among the dancers. As one of the saddest and most beautiful songs begins to play, I cry. Tonio takes pity on me and moves me onto the dance floor. I want to be able to dance flawlessly with him but too many emotions get in the way. He shows unusual kindness to me by letting it pass without comment and I realize I truly wish him well.

Later, Paola arrives to pick me up and we struggle to lift the enormous suitcase onto the back seat. When I manage to shove it onto the Ryanair belt, it clocks in at 34 kilos (75 pounds) – fourteen kilos over the limit. This will cost an additional one hundred thirty euro and I still need to remove one kilo to check the bag! Then the attendant tells me I can bring the extra pounds along for only thirty-three euro if I stuff them into a nylon duffle bag.

* * *

I'm excited to be on my way to Firenze to meet Ray and Carla, my two best friends from California, who I have not seen for one year. I'll be spending the next month with them and an assortment of American friends, in a villa they rented overlooking Lake Trasimeno in Tuscany; acting as interpreter and chef.

* * *

As the plane takes off, I look down at my blonde diamond ring mandala and make a vow to return to Sardinia. And then I make a vow to myself—to be open to receive a deeper kind of love. My journey isn't over, in fact, it may have just begun.

EPILOGUE

During my year of living on Sardinia, I discovered several things about myself:

1. I can feel at home anywhere and living in one place does not suit my nature.
2. Learning a new language after 60 is very hard but possible.
3. My taste in men is changing and sex without love no longer suits me.
4. I am open to meeting a loving life partner.
5. Wherever I go, I *need* to cook for people because feeding others feeds my soul.
6. The social exchange of shopping for local, fresh ingredients and then cooking a meal to share with foreigners who have never tasted that food, is incredibly satisfying for me. I enjoy it as much or more than sampling new foods in a foreign land.

After leaving Sardinia, I joined my California friends, Ray and Carla in a villa they rented in Tuscany for a month. The house was situated on a mountain, overlooking Lake Trasimeno, south of Cortona. It was a treat for me to act as the "house chef" and because I was the only Italian speaker, I did all the translating at the local grocers, fish mongers and butcher shop. As I got to know the butcher and his wife, they began asking questions about how I might prepare recipes with the meats I bought. Of course, they shared their suggestions with me as well, but I never considered how interested these Italians might be in American/Californian cuisine. This inspired me to spend time at a cooking school, which I found near Cortona (and include in my next book). I had not realized how important and integral cooking was in my life until this trip. It was always just something I enjoyed and shared with people but took for granted. Now, I would take it to a whole other level and it made me feel truly excited about my life going forward; more excited than I had felt in many years.

What I could never have guessed about my time abroad is that it would provide a platform for me to earn a living while doing what I love most; traveling, cooking, eating, and experiencing life in new ways. It reminds me of a phrase I used during my years of teaching people how to improve themselves at any age, "It is never too late to begin." I invite you, dear reader, to join me in my travels and share in the unfolding adventures in the coming years. I've got at least ten more good ones left with an equal number of books!

Sperò ci vediamo presto! I hope to see you soon!

ENJOY THE FLAVORS FROM
NOTES FROM A BROAD

You can find many of Zia's recipes mentioned in *Notes From A Broad* by visiting:

www.notesfromabroad.biz

Or, page forward now for three specially selected recipes from Zia's personal collection that you can make today!

ZIA'S STUFFED CARCIOFI WITH TRUFFLE OIL

Ingredients:
> 4 large artichokes, the bigger the better
> 1 T. olive oil for sauté
> 2 T. white truffle oil for stuffing mix
> ½ small yellow onion, chopped small
> 2 medium cloves garlic finely chopped
> 1 C. panko or unseasoned breadcrumbs
> ½ C. grated aged Pecorino cheese
> ¼ C. fresh Italian parsley chopped fine
> ¼ C. fresh Italian basil leaves chopped fine
> ½ C. pine nuts*
> Fresh ground pepper and Truffle Salt to taste

Preparation:

Steam 4 large artichokes and any stems you cut off until barely tender. **Do not overcook** or they will fall apart when stuffed! When cool enough to handle, use a teaspoon to carefully scoop out the choke while leaving the artichoke leaves intact. Set the chokes upright and fairly close together in a shallow ovenproof dish.
Chop the cooked stems very small and put them into a medium-mixing bowl.

Toast the pine nuts a few minutes being careful not to burn them and allow them to cool. Sauté the onion & garlic in olive oil about 5 minutes or until soft, and add to the bowl with chopped stems, pine nuts and all other ingredients. Gently toss together to mix well adding the truffle oil last to moisten the mixture evenly. Using a teaspoon, carefully stuff chokes by dropping the mixture between all layers of leaves and put a teaspoonful in the center.

Bake uncovered at 375 degrees for 20 minutes then turn up the oven to 425 for another 10 minutes or until the tips of chokes barely begin to brown. Serve warm or room temperature on a bed of frisé. The stuffing adheres to the individual leaves as guests peel and enjoy!

*If the pine nuts are tiny, use more.

For an alternate meaty version add cooked crumbles of Italian sausage to the stuffing mix.

THE BLOODY RITA

(Makes about 4 servings depending on the size of the martini glass.)

Ingredients:

4 oz. Heradura Silver or other Blanco Tequila
8 oz. Tomato juice
2 T. olive brine (I use spicy Sicilian Olives)
Juice of half a fresh lime
Freshly grated horseradish to taste (you can garnish with a couple of shavings too).
Spices: fresh cracked pepper, sea salt, Cholula hot sauce and Green Tabasco Sauce

Preparation:

Chill with several ice cubes a few minutes in the shaker and then shake well. Strain into martini glasses with salted rims, a slice of lime and an olive.

FRESH FAVA BEAN AND ARTICHOKE PASTA

Ingredients:
   1 pound (whole pods) fresh fava beans
   1 8-10 oz. jar cooked artichoke hearts (not marinated) drained and sliced into quarters
   1 large yellow onion sliced in rounds and then in half
   2 cloves garlic minced
   1 C. rich chicken or vegetable stock
   ½ C. Vermouth Rosso
   2 C. fresh sheep's milk ricotta cheese
   Extra Virgin Olive oil
   ½ t. hot red pepper flakes (If desired)
   Sea salt to taste
   1 t. Coarse salt
   Fresh cracked pepper
   ½ C. Grated Pecorino cheese (and more for serving)
   ½ C. (uncooked) Penne pasta per person
   Freshly-grated nutmeg (if desired)

Preparation:

Step 1: process Fava beans by popping them out of their pods and plunging the beans into boiling water for a few minutes. Pour into a strainer and when cool enough to handle, pop each bean out of its skin and reserve. *

Step 2: Put the pasta water on to boil. **When it boils**, add a teaspoon of coarse salt to the water before adding the pasta.

Step 3: Heat 3 T. oil in a large heavy skillet on medium and add onion. Add a sprinkle of sea salt, stir and cook slowly 10-15 minutes until they begin to caramelize. Add garlic, red pepper flakes and cook for a few minutes then add artichoke hearts, favas and vermouth. Cook a few minutes more then add stock and cook uncovered until half of the liquid has cooked down. Turn off the heat and add ricotta stirring to just heat through. Taste for salt and add as desired. Add cooked penne and a few tablespoons of the pasta water to the pan and reheat just until hot. Take off the heat again, add the pecorino, stir and serve immediately in pasta bowls. Drizzle a little olive oil and cracked pepper on each serving and more pecorino and nutmeg if desired.

*To easily peel fava beans, cut off the little bump end of the bean and squeeze the other end to pop them out.

Want more from Zia Wesley?
Here's an excerpt from
THE STOLEN GIRL
The Veil and the Crown Series
Book One

Everyone froze in a moment of total silence. Standing in the passageway were two huge, swarthy men with long black hair partially wrapped in dirty turbans and full, unkempt beards. Each held a sword in one hand and a pistol in the other, which they now waved as they screamed something in a language that no one understood. The women shrieked uncontrollably, Aimée slid down the bulkhead to sit upon the floor, still conscious but in shock. The two male passengers backed away from the pirates, spreading their arms protectively in front of the women who huddled behind them. The pirates continued waving their arms and screaming incomprehensible gibberish. Three more pirates entered the salon. Quickly assessing the situation, the five brigands conversed amongst themselves. When their private conversation was finished, they forcibly herded the two men from the room, using their swords to slash at them. The women screamed incessantly as they were physically removed leaving Aimée alone amongst the pirates. Three of them discussed her quietly as they approached where she sat stunned in the corner. They gently lifted her to her feet. She shook uncontrollably, keeping her head down, afraid to look at them, and instinctively covered her bosom with her arms. The pirates exchanged conspiratorial looks as they appraised her, apparently finding her quite desirable. When Aimée found the courage to lift her head and look into their faces, she fainted dead away. However, her direct look gave them a glimpse of her sapphire-blue eyes, which caused a collective gasp.

 Zia Wesley (Wesley-Hosford) is the best-selling author of six books of nonfiction in the genre of health and beauty, and two historical novels published as The Veil and the Crown series; *The Stolen Girl* and *The French Sultana*.

As America's first cosmetics consumer advocate and visionary pioneer of the natural cosmetics industry, Ms. Wesley founded Zia Cosmetics, Inc, and was heralded as "the inspiration of her generation," for teaching women how to turn back the clock on aging. She also danced and sang leading roles in three Broadway shows, practices and teaches Yoga and Pilates, is a master organic gardener, an admired chef, and the grandmother of three young adults.

With this book, Zia hopes to inspire single women of all ages to travel the world on their own terms; to trade their expectations and fears for a deep curiosity for the unknown. She assures the reader that "new adventures bring unexpected experiences and pleasure that keep us young and vibrant."

ENJOY THE PHOTOS AND FLAVORS FROM

NOTES FROM A BROAD
—————◆◆◆◆◆————

You can see Zia's photos of the many places and people mentioned in this book and peruse Zia's original recipes on the website, www.notesfromabroad.biz.

Made in the USA
Middletown, DE
10 November 2019